2025

FINDING *your* DIAMONDS

HEAL THE GIRL AND
THE WARRIOR APPEARS

D1525395

By

LIZ SVATEK

Dedication

To my Grandmother Caroline, who taught me unconditional love.
To my husband, who was my security when I had none.
To my Mother, who decided to heal.
To my son, who started my legacy.
To my daughter Caroline, who will carry it further.
And to "Libba," my little girl, this is all for you.

Table of Contents

Prologue   1

Chapter 1: The Awakening Begins – Is This All There Is?   7

Chapter 2: Healing the Past – Diamonds in the Ashes   25

Chapter 3: Reclaiming Your Power – Boundaries for the Win!   47

Chapter 4: Reframing the Past and Writing Your New Story   75

Chapter 5: Heal the Girl and the Warrior Will Appear   93

Chapter 6: Unleashing Your Inner Warrior by Moving Through Fear   107

Chapter 7: Reinvent, Reclaim, Rise, REPEAT!   119

Chapter 8: Trust the Whisper: Your Intuition is Your Superpower   131

Chapter 9: Designing Your Legacy: Stop Waiting, Start Leading   143

Chapter 10: Becoming HER – Limitless and Unstoppable: Your Next Era 153

Chapter 11: Through the Fire   161

Prologue

Last August I found my legacy in the most unlikely of places; a Taylor Swift concert. Walking into the massive Crypto Arena in Los Angeles, I had no idea what to expect. I wasn't much of a Taylor Swift fan, I knew a few songs, but nothing to really get excited about. My teenage daughter and I were dressed up, had our friendship bracelets on, and were ready to go. In line for the bathroom, a teenager traded bracelets with us and my daughter was thrilled. When I looked into those teenagers' eyes, they were sparkling. For some reason I really took note of that, and I even thought; "Women over forty need to get that sparkle back!"

Later at our seats more and more women and girls were trading bracelets, chatting away, excited, laughing and joyful. "How sweet" I thought. They were playing music in the arena and my daughter informed me that when they played "Applause" by Lady Gaga, the show would be starting. Sure enough when that song came on, everyone started screaming, and a giant countdown clock appeared, projected onto the curtain covering the stage. As the clock counted down, the excitement in the room started to build. I have been to a lot of concerts, but this was nothing like I'd ever felt before. The energy in the room was electric. The joy, freedom and excitement was tangible. It was magic. Suddenly the women in the room were all little girls and teenagers again. Tears came to my eyes, I didn't even know why.

I looked around at the hopeful excited faces of the women and girls around us. Women were holding hands, hugging, crying. As the curtain rose, and the giant flower petals waved, Taylor Swift popped up on a podium. When she started to sing, I realized: we were not at a concert. We were at the women's empowerment superbowl. A love, light and hope festival. We were in a dome of endless possibility, we were LIMITLESS.

In that moment it all became clear. This is what women need right now; love and sisterhood, deep connection, empowerment and community, and a safe place to express all of our emotions and dreams. We need to feel the magic again, the excitement, like a girl in line for the bathroom trading a friendship bracelet. We need that sparkle in our eyes, and we need to connect with the little girls inside of us. That night I saw my legacy. This is what I need to give women. This is who I need to be for women. This is what I need to teach women; that you can have this feeling any time you want. That this feeling has nothing to do with age, or where you live or who you are. You don't even have to like Taylor Swift, but how could you not? Imagine a world where women felt safe, loved, supported and magical. This is the magic of living your legacy NOW.

If you're like me, for years, you did everything "right." You built a life that looked good on paper; a career, marriage, kids, a home. You checked all the boxes, or at least some of them. You sacrificed and put everyone's needs before your own and made sure your family and friends were safe and loved. You've done all the things for all the people. And yet, here you are, staring at the reality of your life at this stage and wondering: Is this it? Is this my life? Is this all there is?

It's not all bad of course, but something feels...off. Maybe you can't even articulate it, but you know it's there. A restlessness. A deep, unshakable yearning for something more. But what is it? You can't quite put your finger on it, so you do what women have been conditioned to do for ages; you push it down, tell yourself to be grateful, and stop complaining. After all, you should be happy, right? Except you're not. Not fully. Not in the way you know you're meant to be. Let me say.... This is GREAT news. Bravo, Queen! Welcome to your awakening.

The Golden Cage of Shoulds

Women in their forties, fifties, and beyond are waking up to a hard truth: We have been living by someone else's rules. We have spent decades carrying the weight of expectations, obligations, and responsibilities. We have been the caregivers, the nurturers, the doers, the fixers. We have prioritized careers, marriages, children, and aging parents, all while putting ourselves last.

And now? Many of us are realizing that we have lost ourselves in the process. We are feeling disconnected, from ourselves, from our friendships, from our partners, and even from the careers and businesses we once loved. We're even disconnected from our bodies and emotions. The tears are stuck in our throats. We have outgrown the lives we've built, and our children have outgrown us, and we don't know what comes next. We are skating on the surface of life, numb, exhausted, weighed down by invisible expectations. We are trapped in the golden cage of shoulds.

You should be grateful.

You should be happy with what you have.

You should stop wanting more.

You should be able to figure this out!

But here's the truth: **You are allowed to want more.** Not more responsibilities. Not more stress. More depth, connection, purpose, and freedom. I wanted all of that, and felt guilty for it. I wanted deeper conversations, more meaningful connection time with family and friends, I wanted to feel like I was living my legacy now; I didn't want to wait for when I was dead and gone, I wanted to truly create a legacy as I was living it. I wanted to feel the feeling you get when your life has meaning and purpose. And...I wanted the freedom to change, and the freedom to say, "I don't want to do this anymore. This is no longer who I am. This is no longer who I want to be."

The Outdated Mid-Life Model

The way mid-life has been sold to us is a lie. We have been conditioned to believe that once we hit forty, we are on a slow, inevitable decline. That mid-life is about settling, shrinking, fading into the background. That it's about focusing on everything we haven't achieved and all the ways we have "failed."

That is bullshit. The model of mid-life we've been given, this outdated, June Cleaver version- was built for a different time; a time when women's roles were limited. It comes from a time when the best we could hope for was pleasing everyone around us and looking good; a time when our worth was measured by how well we served others. That model no longer fits us because, in reality, this time of your life is not a downhill slope; it's the new era of mid-life. This is not the end of something. This is the beginning. This is an ascent. A rocket launch. A rising tide. A phoenix rising. We are not fading. We are expanding. We are not losing value. We are stepping into our highest worth. We are not becoming invisible. We are becoming too bold to be ignored.

The world is also waking up to this. Society is craving depth, meaning, and connection. And women in this season of life? We are the ones who are leading the way. Because we have lived it. We have experienced, learned, struggled, and survived. We have wisdom, and it is our time to rise into impact, to build our legacy, and to fully express who we are without apology.

If you are reading this and you feel the stirrings of something inside you, knowing that you are meant for more, this book is your guide. If you are feeling stuck, unfulfilled, or disconnected, I want you to know that you are not alone. I've not only been there, but I almost stayed there. I also want you to know this: It's normal. This is what is supposed to happen. It's part of your evolution. You are not stuck. You are not lost. You're awakening.

This book is here to show you how to break free from the golden cage, how to release the weight of "shoulds," how to trust yourself again, and how to design a life that feels aligned, powerful, and true. You are moving into a new era. And like Taylor Swift I'm going to take you on my own Eras Tour. I hope through sharing my story of how I found my legacy and purpose, you can find your own. I want you to feel alive again. To feel magical. It's possible, all of it, because you are limitless. We're not waiting anymore for the perfect moment to address all of this. **It's time.**

Chapter 1

The Awakening Begins – Is This All There Is?

*"You've got to live, live, live! Life is a banquet, and most poor
suckers are starving to death!"*

- AUNTIE MAME

I was forty-nine years old, counting down the days to fifty, and I felt like I was drowning. For years, I had been treading water, barely keeping my head above the surface. The weight of everything I carried, expectations, shame, regret, other people's opinions, motherhood, marriage; it was all pulling me under. The only thing keeping me afloat was my outer facade. I was an adorable, well-dressed, drowning person. I clung to this perfectly controlled version of me; the one that made it look easy.

Everyone would tell me that I was a great mom, and I was. I was really there for my kids, except I wasn't really there all the time. The exhaustion, resentment, and questions had built up. I started "faking it," and became a performing puppet, going through the motions, executing the schedules, showing up in all the right places with a sassy smile and self-deprecating joke, but inside I was screaming for an escape. And the more knee deep in volunteering, carpooling, and moms' nights out I was, the more I wanted to crawl out of my skin. And it began when my son came home from the hospital after fifty-two days in the neonatal intensive care unit (NICU).

I will never forget coming home from the hospital with Landon and instead of feeling victorious and excited about finally having my son at home with me, I couldn't help but think, "What have I done?" I was terrified about the gravity of this new role of guiding, raising and loving a child who did not fit the mold that the world expected him to fit. I knew I didn't have a model to do this, that I would be learning as I went. I didn't want my son to have the same childhood I had. I didn't want to be the mother I was raised by. She did the best she could, but I wasn't sure what I had learned that could possibly help me when Landon came home from the NICU. I felt panicked. I wanted to cry out, "I can't do this alone! How is everyone going on with their lives expecting that I know what I'm doing? I have no clue how to do this!" But I held it together the best I could, shoving my fear and lack of know-how down in favor of smiling and hoping things would work out.

I began creating and joining communities of support for myself and for Landon; play groups and play dates, group swim lessons, and Mommy and me classes. I knew I needed wisdom, connection, and support. I wanted both my son and I to be accepted for our differences, his external ones, and my internal ones. He was born with a physical difference, his right arm was far from perfect, and I was far from a perfect mother. Even with all of these groups and support, the loneliest I have ever felt was when I became a mom. Not just those fifty-two days in the hospital, but every morning I woke up and every evening when I realized I had to do it all over again. It was daunting. I felt like I got put into a box and I had no idea how to get out of it.

I didn't know this side of motherhood. The loneliness. The disassociation. The quiet emptiness that I felt right alongside the love, tenderness, and pure joy. I lived for the cozy moments, the ones where my kids and I felt safe, curled up reading books, giggling under the covers, their small hands in mine. But when we were out in the world I felt like no one understood the weight I was carrying. Everyone else seemed content with motherhood; sure they were tired, but they were loving it. I was loving my children, but not loving motherhood. Somewhere along the way, a new feeling crept in. A sinking, gnawing whisper that said, "There's more for you than this." And I panicked. Because mothers aren't supposed to feel that way, right? We're supposed to cherish every second because they're getting older. Every day, hour and minute is something we can't get back so we better be present. We're supposed to live in an emotional scarcity sinkhole, simultaneously soaking in the moment while obsessing over how much we'll miss it when it's gone. Be present. Be patient. Be grateful. Never admit you want something more. Be happy for what you've got! I thought there was something wrong with me.

I had what felt like a bipolar experience of motherhood. One minute, I was fully present, savoring bedtime stories, park picnics, and soul connecting hugs, and the next, I wanted to hand my kids off to a nanny so I could spend the afternoon sipping wine and shopping. And yet, even on the days I did escape, the sinking feeling followed me. The wine and shopping weren't the answer, it was something deeper that I couldn't recognize. I tried to drown it in gratitude. Be grateful. Don't tempt the universe. Your son is alive. Your daughter is healthy. You have a good husband. You have a good life. If you're not grateful enough, it will all be taken away. YOU WANTED THIS. So, I doubled down. I committed harder. I performed and tried to numb the noise of my legacy calling. I had to drown out the feeling that motherhood wasn't enough for me and convince myself that surface conversations were enough. I would look at the moms working full time and act like I felt sorry for them. In reality I was jealous. I wanted permission to be immersed in something other than juice boxes and snack time. I told myself I was better because I was sacrificing. I was putting my kids' needs before my own, I was giving them the childhood I didn't get. I gave them calm, peaceful, and present moments, but inside I was panicking. The silence made the questions I was asking myself even louder. I tried to stay on the surface of everything, avoiding depth at all costs. In depth there was questioning, on the surface there was nothing. Every carpool run, every Parent Teacher Association (PTA) meeting, every home-cooked meal and perfectly curated bedtime routine became a scene in a play starring Liz Svatek as "The Energetic, Devoted, Joyful, Sacrificial Mother!"

I convinced myself that's what being a great mom looked like! Sacrificing my needs. Shrinking my dreams. Pretending that my whole identity, my whole sense of worth, was fulfilled by motherhood alone. I did that until I couldn't pretend anymore, because the truth is motherhood can be deeply meaningful and not enough. You can love your children more than life itself and want something just for you. You can be a great mom and still feel unfulfilled if you're not living your purpose. And that doesn't make you selfish. That makes you human. I wish someone had told me sooner: Wanting more for yourself doesn't mean you want less for your kids. It means you're ready to be fully alive again. It means you're ready for your legacy!

But I didn't know that then. So instead of building a legacy I started building businesses. In the beginning I thought that gave me the meaning and purpose I was lacking, but even when those businesses were successful, I felt guilty for being away from my kids. I still felt like I was chasing the feeling of wanting more. I couldn't find the right combination of being myself, mothering, and impact. Again it seemed like other women had figured this out, but no one was talking about any of it.

I didn't know about the duality of life then. I didn't know life could be both. I didn't know you could want to be a fully present full-time mom and want to live a life of legacy and purpose. I had watched Baby Boom at least fifty times, and I always laughed when Diane Keaton, playing single, working Mom J.C. said to her boss, "I can't have a baby because I have a

12:30 lunch meeting!" I wanted to be in the struggle of balancing two things I wanted and cared about. But I wasn't that fulfilled by my work, so what was my struggle? Why was I having this feeling? I was so intent on mothering differently, being focused and all in on my children. I wanted them to feel seen, heard, and validated, and it had become a full-time job. I was afraid for my kids to feel the way I had; lonely and scared, and yet I was feeling those same feelings again, like there was no one to turn to, to tell the truth to, and to love me through this.

Meanwhile, I kept searching for the escape hatch that didn't exist. I needed to find the trap door on the stage floor where I could bow out, just for a little while. Would anyone even notice if I disappeared? Maybe my identical twin could take over the show while I snuck off to Maui? Too bad I don't have a twin...I kept waiting for someone to step in, for someone to see how exhausted I was and say, "Hey, I got this, take a break." But no one was coming. Because this was my life. And I had asked for this. I had signed up for this marriage, this family, this career. This relentless, all-consuming performance of "having it all together." But still, I kept wondering, when would I get a moment to just breathe? Like, really breathe. Because I never did. I was always holding my breath. I come from a long line of breath holders. Sitting next to my father on the couch as a kid, I would hear it, the sudden, audible exhale that broke the silence. Not a sigh. Not relief. More like survival; it was a momentary gasp for air before he went back under. Was he waiting for his escape too? At six years old, I started holding my breath, and there I was, almost fifty years old, still waiting to breathe.

I couldn't be the only one feeling this way, I thought. *I mean, surely other women felt this way too, right?* My friends and I would all laugh about the exhaustion, the endless to-do lists, the way we could recite our kids' schedules better than our own dreams. We were always juggling work and recitals. But deep down, did we all feel that ache? Were we all asking

=

ourselves if this was it? If it was all enough? So, I started testing the waters. It was easier with a glass of pinot grigio in hand, the clink of wine glasses filling the gaps in our conversations. Wine nights had a rhythm- complaints, laughter, more wine, maybe some gossip, and an unspoken agreement that no one really told the truth. But one night, between refilling glasses, I said it. "Do you ever think about what's next? Like... when the kids are older? What do we actually want to do with our lives?" The room went silent. One mom stared into her glass like it held the answer. Another shifted uncomfortably in her chair. Someone let out a forced laugh.

"Oh my god, Liz. Can we not? We're finally relaxing," said one of the moms I wasn't very close to. And just like that, the moment passed and my heart deflated. Someone made a joke about husbands who couldn't find anything in the fridge. Someone else talked about a new workout class that was supposed to change everything. The conversation slipped back into safe territory, like my question had never happened. I smiled, took a sip, and laughed at the jokes, but inside, something cracked. Because if I had to cover that question with another joke, if I had to shove my truth back down with another sip of wine, what else was I avoiding? And that's when I noticed that I wasn't just holding my tongue. **I was holding my breath...again.**

I was holding my breath with my kids, hoping nothing bad would happen. I was holding my breath in my marriage, hoping we could stay together. I was holding my breath until bedtime so I could be alone, so that I could worry in silence instead of with everyone talking all around me. I was always holding my breath, waiting to feel something other than exhaustion and overwhelm, but of course that never happened. I was holding my breath all the damn time. Turns out I had a real chip on my shoulder. I was totally embracing and glorifying the masculine energy of pushing through, forcing things, and not asking for help. I wanted to be the best mother, have the best marriage, and the most successful business, but I was always failing at one of them. Why couldn't I figure this out? I remembered how many times my father had tried to toughen me up. "Stop being such a wimp," was one of his go-to phrases.

If other mothers were struggling, I would be right there with love and guidance, but I believed I had to have it all together. I didn't want anyone to judge me. I wouldn't let anyone see me drowning, or speak about it in any real way. Instead, my friends and I would complain, joke, and drink more wine. That was the socially acceptable way to handle things. We weren't miserable, we were just "crazy busy" moms. We didn't want more, we were just tired. We didn't want to be seen and heard and validated, we were just pissed at the moms who weren't volunteering because how dare they have boundaries or a life. We didn't want to pursue our own dreams, we wanted our kids to have their dreams. Besides, we could just blame our husbands for our unhappiness. That was always an easy, deflective target.

But as the years went by, and the kids got older, more and more truth was leaking out. Between glasses of wine I would start saying how I was really feeling. I was getting emotional, looking at the depth of where I was, and I would always get looks from my friends. They would empathize and sympathize to a point, but they were drowning too. I'm sure they were wishing I would just stop and go back to the comfortable conversations, and their disapproving looks would cause me to retract and shove everything back down. I would make a joke, plaster a smile on my face, and move on.

Even the wine, my little helper, wasn't helping much anymore. One glass wasn't cutting it, I needed another, and another...that first sip of wine was deceiving, it seemed like it helped make it all go away, but it never got better than the first sip. I'd need a whole bottle to drown this feeling out; this emptiness, loneliness, this feeling of living the same day over and over again...I couldn't hide from it all anymore. I kept going to the regular moms' night outs, the wine infused gatherings, drinking more to numb out my feelings. Meanwhile I began to feel even worse about myself.

=

I was like a boat taking on water. I couldn't stop it all from coming in. I was going under. Like a kid learning to swim, the only thing above water was my face; gasping for air, just enough to survive. I was always panicking because I knew the air was running out. And yet, interestingly enough, I couldn't feel it in my body. There was no rush of adrenaline, no heart-pounding panic, no fight-or-flight response kicking in. Just... nothing. An eerie stillness. A terrifying kind of silence. The kind my friends and I would try to outrun by staying insanely busy and drinking many bottles of wine.

"I'm just so crazy busy," I would say when people asked how I was. "You know how it is." And everyone nodded. Because every woman I knew was crazy busy and we were not about to tell our secrets of our drowning. Instead we wore our "crazy busy" titles like badges of honor, proud of the fact that we were doing it all. In reality, we had a lump in our throats and a weight the size of a piano on our backs.

The truth was that I wasn't as busy as I was numb. There's a difference. The busyness was inside. It was a non-stop humming, like a motor that kept me going, but it felt like I was trying to make it through a swamp. Murky and muddy, I just trudged through and tried to make it look easy so that other moms would be impressed. I was stuck in autopilot, though, because I had been there for so long. The longer I showed up the way I thought I should, smiled the way I thought I should, and said the things I thought I should, the less I could feel much of anything. I couldn't feel sadness, anger, panic...I couldn't even feel joy.

For many of us, myself included, mid-life is challenging beyond the physical changes. If you have children, once they get older, your role starts to change. Kids or no kids, we start thinking about the trajectory of our lives. We find ourselves standing on the metaphorical rooftop of our existence, surveying everything that has happened; the choices, the compromises, the victories, and the heartbreaks. It's as if we've been climbing a staircase in the dark for years, step by step, and suddenly someone flips the light switch. We see it all. The patterns. The wounds. The beliefs that were never ours to begin with. And most importantly, the parts of ourselves we lost along the way.

Awakening in your forties, fifties, or even sixties isn't about having a single a-ha moment where everything magically makes sense. It's more like The Truman Show, remember that 1998 movie where Jim Carrey's character, Truman Burbank, slowly starts noticing cracks in his perfectly curated world? At first, it's subtle. A light falls from the "sky," and then a radio station describes his exact movements in real-time. Then, he notices the same people passing him at the same time every day. The illusion starts to crumble, but he's not quite sure what to do with it. That's how awareness came to me in mid-life.

At first, the signs were small for me. I started questioning things that once felt normal. Why do I feel so impatient and annoyed with these conversations about diet, fashion, and exercise? Why do I keep saying yes to going out when my entire body wants to say no? Why does this job feel so boring and meaningless? Am I actually good at anything? What am I supposed to be doing? Why does this version of my life suddenly feel too tight, like a sweater two sizes too small? Why do I feel so stuck, alone and afraid? These questions first came in whispers, but anytime I tried to ignore them they got louder.

The universe nudges us, and if we still refuse to look, it sometimes shoves us, and sometimes knocks us over with a crisis we can't ignore, burnout, divorce, a health scare, or an unshakable sense of dissatisfaction. And when that happens we are forced to choose ourselves. Sometimes, for the first time ever. But even when there isn't an impending crisis, the first step in reclaiming ourselves is always awareness. We can't fix what we don't see. But here's the thing: awareness happens in stages.

=

At first, I looked back at certain moments in my life and thought, who is this woman? Where have I gone? What happened to the carefree, confident woman who moved to Los Angeles knowing no one? What happened to the version of me who left her boyfriend behind to follow her dreams? I put my dreams and desires first back then. I remember sitting in my new one-bedroom apartment in the Hollywood Hills, that I had no clue how I would afford, with my cat Scooter. I had a mattress on the floor and a velvet bench that was it. I had gone to a cool furniture store on La Brea and bought a gold velvet baroque bench. Nothing I did back then was practical or realistic, it was all based on my desires and what I truly wanted. I had a view of the whole city from my apartment. Even then, with the few things that I had, I felt like I made it. So what the actual hell happened to her?

I was watching my life like a TV show. Little by little, the patterns I was repeating started revealing themselves, the constant people-pleasing, the way I would say yes to every volunteer opportunity no matter how exhausted I was, the over-functioning and worrying, and the way I would try to be perfect at everything. It showed up in the way I kept refusing to address my own needs, and prioritizing everything and everyone else, but never felt like I was doing enough. It showed up in the way I honored sacrificing, but felt resentful and angry all the time. It was all starting to add up. And then, like a lightning bolt, the truth hit me: I couldn't do it anymore.

This is where things got really uncomfortable because once I saw it, I couldn't unsee it. Just like Truman in *The Truman Show* when he realized he lived on a set and not in the real world. Once the illusion was broken, once I saw my life for what it was instead of what I'd been telling myself it was, I couldn't go back. And it was scary and dark because I had no idea what this was going to look like. I was venturing into unknown territory.

I know now that awareness is when the real magic begins. Awareness, as uncomfortable as it is, is a gift. It means we're no longer sleepwalking through our lives. It means we're standing on that rooftop, looking at everything we've built, and asking, what do I want to keep? What do I want to tear down? It's the moment we realize we get to decide who we want to be for the rest of our lives. And once we have that realization, the next step is inevitable: we start making changes.

It was Christmastime 2018 and I was meticulously planning the perfect holiday. I poured so much energy into crafting the perfect holiday card. That will make me feel better, I told myself. I carefully chose our color-coordinated outfits, rich eggplant purple and soft greys to match our amethyst-colored couch. I made sure both of my kids looked polished, told them to sit up straight, and smoothed out every wrinkle. When they smiled, I coached them. "No, not like that. A real smile. Like this." I flashed a perfect grin, desperate for the illusion to be real. If I take this perfect picture, maybe I can believe in the facade, I told myself. Look at everything you have. Everything is great. Look how lucky you are, I reminded myself as the photographer got us into place.

A few weeks later, the pictures arrived from the photographer, and as expected, they were flawless. The lighting, the angles, the color palette, everything was perfect. For a brief moment, I felt relief. See? This is it. You made it. You have it all. When people saw this card, they would see a happy family, a beautiful life, a woman who had it all together. And for a fleeting moment, I almost believed it myself.

I was so ahead of schedule that I ordered the cards early. When they arrived, I held one in my hands, admiring the crisp design, the elegant font, and the polished smiles. It was so perfect, in fact, that I decided to frame it. But as I slipped the picture inside, locked up the back levers, and turned it over, I saw it. Something dark. I leaned in, trying to dismiss the unsettling feeling creeping up my spine. What is that? I tried to wipe it away in my mind, to brush it aside like a smudge on glass. But then I saw it. The fear in our eyes. My eyes. My husband's. My children. We didn't look joyful.

=

We didn't look happy. We looked like people running for their lives, desperate to uphold an illusion, terrified that someone might see the truth. We were not okay.

Could anyone else see it? Would they notice the overly polished smiles, the stick-straight posture, the way I orchestrated my children to unknowingly play along, absorbing the script I had been writing for years? Standing in my perfect living room of my new, perfect house, the tears I had been shoving down for years crawled up my throat. I swallowed them back. *No. I am not going to deal with this, not right now. I worked too hard for this picture. It took twelve years to create this moment. I refuse to let the shame and guilt take me down.*

But it was too late. The truth had already cracked the surface. I wasn't just wearing a mask, I had built an entire world around it. And the worst part? I used my husband and children to do it. And just like that, the illusion shattered. The awareness hit. The light switch flipped. I could no longer pretend I didn't see it.

I just wanted a win...how had this happened? Looking back now, I feel so much sadness for the woman I was then. And if I'm being honest, I also want to judge her. I want to shake her by the shoulders and ask, "Why didn't you see what you were doing? Why couldn't you have realized this sooner? Why couldn't you just be a better mother?" But I know the answer. And when I allow myself to really see her, to see me, the compassion floods in. Because I imagine my forty-year-old self looking at me, exhausted, and pleading, "Can't you see how hard I'm trying? I don't know what else to do." I can see her, trying so hard to push the feelings down, and living for that glass of wine at the end of the night.

She was constantly looking for the reward for all her self-sacrifice. She wanted to be everything, a good mom, a good wife, and a good person. She wanted to be the kind of person everyone admired, the one who made it look effortless. But when you're inside the wine bottle, you can't read the label, and that version of myself? She was not ready to read the label that was staring at her. She had survived the kind of birth story people whisper about, the kind you don't tell at baby showers. And after that, all she wanted was a win. Just one. She was desperate for a moment where she could feel like she was doing it right, where life didn't feel like a never-ending game of catch-up. So she tried to control what was never hers to control...her children's happiness, their self-worth, their love for her, her husband's confidence, his fulfillment, his love for her, what her friends thought, what her family thought, what anyone thought. As if, by managing it all perfectly, she could finally silence the voice in her head that kept asking, "Will I ever be enough?"

I thought I had checked all the boxes. Awesome wife. Dedicated mother. Tireless volunteer. Community-building PTA president. Entrepreneur. On paper, it looked like I had won. But in reality? It all felt empty. I was there, but I wasn't really there. I was with my kids, but I was counting the minutes until I could finally have a second to myself. I was present, but resentful. And I had found all the socially acceptable ways to stay busy, ways that made me look good, that made me feel like I was doing something important, and that made sure I never had to sit still long enough to admit I was unhappy. Because that realization? It scared the hell out of me. Because if I admitted I wanted more, I would have to admit that what I had wasn't enough. I would have to admit that something inside of me was breaking. And I would have to do something about it.

I wish I could tell you that right then and there, when I saw that Christmas card, I made a decision. I wish I could say that this was my moment of transformation, the low point that catapulted me into change. But no. I didn't want to admit it, accept it, or even begin to figure out how to change it. Fear grabbed me by the throat. It told me that if I started making changes, everything would fall apart. So, I poured my usual glass of wine and shoved it down. The truth is, change only happens when

=

you're committed. You're either committed, or you're just interested, and I don't even know if I was interested at that point if I'm being honest. I was scared, that much I know for certain. If you're committed, you follow through whether you feel like it or not. You show up messy, exhausted, and doubting if anything will work, but you still show up. You still do the work.

If you're just interested in change, or so terrified of it like I was, you're not committed. You may try to make some changes but, in the end, nothing happens. You may read the books, save the inspirational quotes, or maybe even have the conversation, but you'll keep waking up in the same life, waiting for the right moment, the right motivation, the right sign, unless you really commit. And, like most women, I only committed when it became too painful to do anything else. That's what they don't tell you about transformation; it's not always a grand moment of clarity. Sometimes, it's just the slow erosion of everything that no longer fits until you're forced to finally make a choice, and when the fear of staying the same becomes greater than the fear of change.

No, the breaking point for me didn't come right away. It crept up slowly, disguised as exhaustion, irritability, and a low-grade dissatisfaction that I kept brushing aside. At first, I wasn't ready to admit anything needed to change. I was still trying to outrun my own truth. I told myself I was just tired, that this was just life, that maybe I was expecting too much. I stayed busy, filling my days with obligations, to-do lists, and commitments that made me look like I had it all together. But at night, when everything was quiet, that voice inside me whispered, is this really it? And every time it did, I shushed it, because answering that question would mean admitting that something wasn't right. And if I admitted that, I'd have to do something about it.

Deep down I felt like a fraud. I knew I was living a lie but I didn't know how to live anything else. The awareness I was having wasn't enough anymore. I was feeling the need to out myself, to tell the truth about my life, and make changes. Like a frog in hot water, I was reaching the boiling point. Nothing was feeling good anymore. I couldn't make the magic happen in my life anymore because I realized it was all a facade. None of it even mattered. The clothes, the pictures, the way it looked. Who was I living for? Whose life was this? Did it matter how it looked to everyone else when I wasn't happy?

At first, it was easy for me to stay in this phase, to ignore the nagging feeling that something was missing. It was easy to gaslight myself into believing that I was just ungrateful, that I should be happy, that what I had was enough, and to stay stuck, waiting for something external to give me permission to want more. But I was starting to realize that permission was never coming. The truth was that it felt safer to feel all of this than do anything about it. It felt more comfortable to stay in the mess than find a way out. But eventually the water comes to a boil, and the frog wants out.

For me, that moment came on my forty-ninth birthday. I woke up and realized I was a year away from turning fifty. I looked at my life and felt like I had hit a wall. I couldn't keep going the way I was living. I was exhausted on a soul level. I couldn't take one more step as the person I was becoming. The reality was that the clock was ticking. A whole forty-nine years had passed with me at the bottom of the list behind my husband, my kids, my family, my work, and my friends...I was prioritizing everyone and everything above myself. At that point, I don't even think I was on the list.

I watched other women around me turning fifty, and instead of celebrating, they were hiding it. No one wanted to admit they had reached this milestone age, not because they feared getting older, but because they felt like I felt: there was nothing to celebrate. They believed, like I did, that they had nothing to show for all those years that made them feel proud. We had lost our value, or so we believed. Somewhere along the way, we had let our dreams fall away, our passions die, our wants and needs fade into the background. We had become too busy taking care of everyone

=

else, running around, making sure everything went smoothly, and when we finally had a moment to ourselves, there was nothing left. We had put our dreams on hold for so long they now seemed irrelevant or childish.

I started dreading the gatherings with the women I had always spent time with. I remember sitting in rooms filled with conversations about kids, husbands, work, and nothing else. It was like we were a bunch of women who didn't exist beyond our roles. We were in support of everyone else's dreams, with no dreams of our own. And if I did meet a woman who was actively living life on her terms, I was jealous. I was jealous of her passion and her direction, because I had neither. I didn't have anything I was excited about. That day, on my forty-ninth birthday, I knew I couldn't keep living like that. The pain of being a year away from turning fifty and still living a dreamless existence was too heavy.

So, I made a decision. I was going to commit to changing myself. I didn't care what I had to do, I was going to do it. I refused to slink into fifty feeling like I had been a spectator in my own damn life. I didn't know exactly what needed to change, but I knew one thing: I was done pretending. I was done shrinking. I was done settling for a life that looked good on the outside, but felt like nothing on the inside. I decided I didn't want more stuff. I wanted more *me*. No more drowning. No more numbness. No more living on autopilot. I was going to feel alive again. I was done settling and done saying I was fine when I wasn't. I was done pretending that joy was something I could live without. I was done letting my life lead me instead of stepping up and leading it myself. I was ready to take radical personal responsibility for my life, and it's time for you to do the same.

Awareness is the first step of every transformation. You cannot change what you refuse to acknowledge, and you cannot rise from a life you've numbed your way through. So many women spend years on autopilot like I did, doing what's expected, staying busy, pushing through, without ever pausing to ask: Is this even the life I want? But the moment you become aware, the moment you name the deepest longings of your soul, the dissatisfaction, and the ache for more, is the moment everything begins to shift. Awareness isn't weakness; it's power. It's the crack in the armor that lets your truth finally shine through. These next reflections are designed to help you tune in, tell your truth, and begin the most important conversation of your life, the one with yourself.

Exercises & Reflections to Break Through the Fog & Step into Awareness

Exercise 1: The "Fine vs. Fantastic" Inventory

Life over forty can feel like a slow settling, a quiet agreement that this is just how life is. But is that actually true? Let's find out.

Grab your journal and make two columns:

Column 1: What in my life feels just fine (neutral but not great, routine, autopilot)?

Column 2: What in my life feels fabulous (energizing, fulfilling, joyful)?

Look at the "fine" column and ask yourself the following questions:

- Am I just going through the motions here?
- Is this an area where I've been settling instead of choosing?
- What would make this feel more fulfilling? Even if the answer feels impossible, write it anyway.

Look at the "fabulous" column and ask yourself:

- Why do these areas feel different?
- What about them makes me feel fully alive?
- How can I bring more of this energy into the areas that feel fine?

=

Reflection:

Settling happens so subtly we don't even realize we've stopped asking for more. What's one area of your life where you know you've settled but deep down, you want more? Write it down. No judgment. Just the truth.

One day, you wake up and realize "fine" isn't cutting it anymore. You've checked all the boxes, played all the roles, and followed the script, yet here you are, wondering, is this really it?

It's time to stop settling for "fine" and start demanding extraordinary things.

That feeling, that whisper, isn't a sign that you're ungrateful. It's a sign that your soul is calling for more. It's your legacy calling. And the moment you hear that call, you have two choices: Ignore it and keep treading water, gasping for air, trying to survive, or...you answer it. At forty-nine, I chose to answer it. And if you're reading this, I have a feeling you're ready too. **Buckle up, Warrior Woman, your reinvention starts now.**

Chapter 2

Healing the Past –
Diamonds in the Ashes

*"You can't connect the dots looking forward; you can only
connect them looking backwards. So you have to trust that the
dots will somehow connect in your future."*

- STEVE JOBS

I f you're going to reinvent yourself, you have to take a little trip down
memory lane, and yes, I know, some of those streets have potholes the
size of Texas. But here's the deal: There's no skipping over it, no detour,
no more saying, "I'd rather not, thanks." You have to go through it, sift
through it, like you're panning for treasure amongst the mud, because
buried in the ashes of your past are diamonds; the wisdom, the lessons, the
strength...those are *diamonds* that you didn't even know you were
collecting.

Why are the hard things we've been through diamonds? Think about
it. Diamonds are formed under extreme pressure, buried deep beneath the
earth, they endure intense heat, time, and transformation before they
shine. Just like that diamond, the hardest, most painful moments of your
life have the potential to shape your deepest wisdom. What felt like
destruction may have been the pressure that revealed your brilliance.
These are the diamonds in the ashes of your past hurts and struggles; they

are unexpected gifts born from the fire. Looking for the diamonds in your past is how you learn to let go of what is no longer serving you and step into the powerful woman you really are.

The past is where we quietly absorbed the beliefs and stories that shaped how we see ourselves and the world. It's where so many of us learned, often without realizing, that love sometimes came with conditions, that success required self-sacrifice, and that worthiness was tied to how much we gave, not how we felt inside. These lessons weren't always taught with words, they were modeled by the adults in our lives, and we absorbed them and believed them; never questioning or doubting our mothers or their mothers. But the truth is that we don't have to keep living by those old rules. When we begin to gently examine the past with compassion, we can start to reclaim what still serves us and release what doesn't. It's like walking through a home you once lived in, cherishing the memories and moments that matter, and choosing to leave behind the things that no longer belong to the life you're building now. This is how you design your life versus having your life lead you.

I have had so many of my clients tell me, with a confident shrug, "Oh, I had a great childhood, I was lucky." And then, upon further reflection, they suddenly say, "Oh yeah, my parents ignored all my emotional needs because my brother was a star athlete," or "I was rewarded for being perfect so I didn't tell them about what was really going on," or "I basically raised myself while my mom drank Chardonnay and watched soap operas." Many of us grew up in homes that looked great on the outside, or seemed normal to us, but had a plot twist inside. The family photos were flawless, the Christmas cards were on point, but, behind the scenes, a lot of us were starring in a psychological thriller no one warned us about, myself included.

Most women who I work with want to be grateful, respectful, and fair, especially to their parents, and I understand that urge. We want to remember the pretty picture we grew up in, or paint the picture to look nicer than it actually felt, but if we're being honest, most of us grew up raising ourselves in some way. Some of the most successful and capable women I know were parentified as kids, meaning they had to step in to support their parents in one way or another when they were far too young to do so. While other children were playing, they were busy being their parents' friend, supporter, advocate, or therapist, providing emotional or practical support far beyond their years. Some of these seemingly meaningless conversations changed who we were as little girls. When adults go to little girls for advice, or for a sympathetic ear regarding adult issues, those little girls start stepping in as caregivers. This is the signature of a stolen childhood. Burdening a child with adult matters and dysfunction, instead of letting them be free. No wonder women who were raised this way come to me for coaching feeling burnt out, overworked, and stressed. They've had a job since they were five, and I can relate to them; I was them.

My parents did the best they could, but, as we all know, no parent can meet all of their children's needs. Every generation of parenting is an evolution, learning more about what children really need to grow up feeling safe, seen, and valued. Family is supposed to be our first experience of home, the place where we learn love, safety, and belonging. But for me, family felt more like a battlefield; one I had to carefully navigate, avoiding emotional landmines while trying to figure out who I was in the process.

I grew up thinking love and safety were rare commodities, so I became the queen of walking on eggshells. I learned to anticipate emotions before they exploded, to keep the peace at all costs, and to make myself smaller, better, or funnier if it meant avoiding conflict. That kind of survival mode didn't just magically turn off when I grew up. It followed me into adulthood, into my relationships, into my career, until I finally woke up and realized I didn't have to live like that anymore. That's the gift of looking back. The purpose is not to blame or to wallow, but to finally understand; to see the patterns for what they are, to rewrite the story, and to reclaim

=

myself in the process. Because I finally realized that reinvention wasn't about becoming someone new, it was about returning to the little girl I was, before I was burdened by the needs of other people. So, if I was going to get serious about reinvention, I knew it was time to stop minimizing, sugarcoating, or pretending that my childhood was anything other than what it was. I had to take a long hard look at my past and learn from it. I had to take the diamonds and leave the rest.

My dad was a rebel, a man who was already enlisted in the military when he quickly married a woman he barely knew, likely trying to do a good deed as she was pregnant with me. He went to Vietnam fully expecting to die, and in some ways, the man who returned was not the same one who had left; part of him did die there. He came back with Post Traumatic Stress Disorder (PTSD) and an even more violent temper, carrying the weight of his own traumatic and violent upbringing. My mother and I bore the brunt of that rage. His unpredictable, volatile nature shaped my entire childhood, and I never knew which version of him would walk through the door. I was on guard, slowly taking on his PTSD with every violent outburst. I was an innately joyful kid; like a little buoy that kept popping back up, no matter what. But he couldn't stand that light. He wanted to hold me under, to drown what refused to dim. After all, I was the one who threw a wrench into my parents' already fragile dynamic. My dad never expected to survive Vietnam, and my mom was supposed to marry a gentleman from a wealthy family, not Danny Zucco from *Grease*.

I was living in a volatile house with two young parents trying to get to know each other, ignoring their trauma and pain, all while raising a baby. This was not the magic combination for a great childhood. I don't have a ton of memories from my childhood. I see the pictures and I look happy, but my father never smiled. He looked like he was drowning, weighed down by it all. Most of my fondest memories are of times with my grandmother. There were magical moments when she would spend time with me, or take me to the playground, or to a museum. I don't have a lot of memories of anything else. It turns out there's a reason for that; you have to feel safe to make memories. If you're living in fight or flight, your body can't store them. You're too busy surviving, and I was definitely surviving.

My father began to scare me more and more. It seemed like I was constantly "in trouble," for what I can't imagine or recall. I was a funny, obedient, and creative kid, but somehow I was always making him angry. Just him coming at me with an accusation sent terror down my spine, and urine down my legs. I would be so afraid of his "spankings," I became desperate and would beg and cry before it even began. The look in his eyes, the rage and anger, I'll never forget it. I began to realize I was living with an emotional terrorist. My mother did try sometimes to come to my defense, but there was no stopping him. He would become more angry, more aggressive, and she would be frozen in fear. I began to believe I was on my own. My grandmother didn't live close, so I had no one to help me. One of the reasons I came to love writing was because I wrote so many letters to my Grandmommie. I loved getting her letters in the mailbox because they were proof that hope existed.

Eight years after I made my entrance to this world, my sister was born. This time my parents were having a planned child, and she was welcomed into a home where my father had mellowed a bit. He began to be more depressed than angry. He gained weight and would eat meals in bed watching TV, and tune out. He was lost. Still, my sister witnessed, at a very young age, his violence and rage towards me and my mother. He never directed his anger at her, but she was there. She was feeling those same feelings of fear, having no idea what to do with it. I was excited to have a sister in the beginning; she was adorable and fun. I thought this might make us a family, and somehow pull us together by bringing love into the house, but I was wrong.

=

My father controlled everything. How the money was spent, social plans, even decorating. It was like my Mother didn't exist. On a trip to visit my grandmother, my father decided to gut the kitchen and start a re-model. Upon our return, we walked in the kitchen and looked around in shock. He didn't care about our reaction or the kitchen being unusable; he just did as he pleased. I remember my mother in tears. One time he "cleaned out the basement" and threw out all her art supplies. She cried and cried. There seemed to be no end to his cruelty.

My mother was somewhat affectionate, but always distant and dis-tracted by the internal and external chaos. She was dodging the bullets of his anger, and wanting him to love her all at the same time. My parents rarely said "I love you," not to each other, and not to me or my sister. There were not many moments of comfort or affirmation for her or me. My mom was young, overwhelmed, and caught in the constant storm of my father's unpredictable rage. When my mom was pregnant with my sis-ter, she nearly died during childbirth, and after that, something changed. She became totally immersed and enamored with my sister, pouring en-ergy into her in a way she never had with me. The difference was stark and painful. I could feel the resentment toward me, and the undercurrent of disappointment. My sister represented hope for the future, I represented the pain of the past; that's the narrative that developed in my mind slowly, but surely, over time.

As a teenager, I had never been able to pin down where this resent-ment from my mother was coming from. I was having lunch with my mother one day, and I literally asked myself, *why would a mother resent her child?* The words came out of my mouth.

"Was I a surprise?"

"Yes, you were," she answered and told me about how she had no idea what she was doing back then. "Your father couldn't even see you until you were six months old," she said, "And when he returned from Vietnam we were just trying our best to make it work." Finally things were starting to make sense. I felt justified after all the gaslighting and telling me that it wasn't true that she loved my sister more than me. The fact was that she did. She couldn't help herself. I was the death of her dreams, and my sister was a new future. I was a punishment; she had made her bed, and had to sleep in it. I started to believe that I was unwanted, and because I was unwanted, I needed to prove my worth even more. And I did.

By the time I was a teenager, my parents' marriage had collapsed under the unending weight of dysfunction, and I became the emotional caretaker for my mother. My dad was actively trying to destroy my mother with his new weapon: money. Financial abuse is one of the least talked about forms of abuse, but it leaves huge scars. After sixteen years of marriage where she was verbally abused, he wouldn't leave her with an ounce of dignity, or money, which was a breaking point for her mentally.

Soon after they split up, my father began dating the sister of a girl I practically worshiped in high school. She was in her young twenties. This family was the blonde version of the Kennedys; sporty, great looking, and preppy with the biggest house in the neighborhood. I was humiliated as word spread around my high school about my dad. I remember going to dinner with him and his "girlfriend" months later, and liking her, but wondering what the hell she was doing with my Dad. But truthfully, I had no time for that. At fifteen years old I was suddenly and officially in charge, although I had been taking care of both of my parents emotionally since I was five. But now, with my mother so depressed that she was physically unable to get out of bed, I had to step up even more, not just for myself, but for my sister. I had to keep up the facade, keep things together, and make sure my sister was protected in a way no one had ever protected me.

I was resentful of my father, but I was glad he was leaving. There was no place to feel safe in the house unless he was gone. I was sick of watching him treat my mother so badly and I was starting to speak up more and

=

more. When they both came into my room to "announce" they were divorcing, I was not surprised. He did all the talking, of course, acting like he was a fallen hero. My mother was quietly crying in the background looking completely defeated. I remember looking into his eyes, interrupting his diatribe about this being "for the best," and simply told him, "Get out." It was one of the few times I could safely stand up to my father. In my mind, I was done with him even if she wasn't.

My sister needed me more than ever, but I resented her too. I didn't want to protect her; I needed protection. She was my mother's wanted child, my father's pal, and my burden now. While I had always been naturally nurturing in my friendships and relationships, my sister felt different. I felt sorry for her being caught up in this family of dysfunction, but I had to swim and keep myself alive. I couldn't let her pull me under. Her innocence bothered me because I wanted it so badly. *When did I have that? When did I get to be innocent and free?* I had been holding this family together for years, and this buoy was tired. I knew how to keep everything running, keep everyone happy, and keep us from falling apart. I was proud of that, but now I didn't want to know what I knew. I wanted to be a kid again; I wanted to get a do-over for all the childhood I lost on the battlefield.

I minimized my childhood trauma for years, especially to myself. I told myself the good parts of my story and ignored what it was like to live in it. No one would have known all this was going on. From the outside looking in, my father was seen as successful, charismatic, a man who had climbed the corporate ladder, even making it into Wharton School in Pennsylvania after returning from Vietnam. People thought he was impressive and accomplished, but in truth, he wasn't as well liked if you really knew him. He could impress a stranger or acquaintance, but those who knew him well felt the raging undercurrent. I wanted my father to love me, and when he was loving towards me, it felt powerful. I lived for those moments, begged for them even. He would make the other parents laugh, and I would laugh too. I would set up his jokes and stories for him, and compliment him in front of others because that's what he liked. I loved to make him smile and laugh. I lived for it. Back at home I was either ignored, targeted, or hiding from him.

Behind closed doors, there wasn't much laughter. We were just survivors. I learned to be the good girl, the one who didn't cause trouble, who avoided the wrath of my father by anticipating what would set him off before it happened. I would sneak through the heavily landmined battlefield hoping to not get blown up. I started staying away from the house as much as I could when I was old enough. I felt like I was raising myself, with no one to ask questions to or get guidance from. I began to believe I was great at handling it all, I didn't need anyone's help. I had learned that emotions weren't safe because I was not allowed to express them at home.

Thank God for my "Grandmommie," the one person who was always looking out for me. She was by my mother's side when I was born, and while my father was deployed. Grandmommie was the first person to show me what unconditional love looked like. She saw me for who I really was, told me I was special, noticed every little thing I did and felt. She could hold space for my emotions, and in her arms I was safe. She was my lifeline, the person who made me feel important, and loved. And yet, despite that, the messages I received at home took root deep inside me.

I learned that it was crucial to watch out and stay vigilant because something might happen. *Be ready.* My father's rage taught me that at any moment, the rug could get pulled out from under me. I had to be prepared. Worrying was the way I could stay prepared. Mistakes were unforgivable. I could be doing something "wrong" without realizing it and my world would fall apart. The consequences were dire. I had to do everything perfectly and make no mistakes. I had to earn love and safety. I worked hard to be "good," to avoid setting him off, to make sure I wasn't the reason for the next explosion. I became a woman who worked hard to earn everyone's love; family, friends, coworkers, it didn't matter who it was, I had to accommodate them.

Loyalty was everything to my father and yet he was disloyal to us. Lying was the biggest offense in my father's eyes; there was no greater form of disrespect. Even when I told the truth, sometimes he thought I was lying, so I would tell him the lie he wanted to hear. I knew that there needed to be joy and humor in the house, so I became a little stand up comedian. I believed it was my job to bring levity. I was naturally funny, a great storyteller like my father, and I found humor in everything I possibly could. My mother would ask for me to tell certain stories over and over to cheer her up. I told funny stories about what was happening in our lives and my life outside of our home. I had great timing, knew when to hit each joke, and how to riff and ad-lib on the spot. And when there was nothing to laugh about, I embellished. My dad loved a good story, and would often say, "Don't let the facts get in the way of a good story." It was such confusing messaging; isn't embellishing lying? And lying is wrong...right? I was getting mixed messages all the time. I never knew the rules of the game I was playing. They seemed to change all the time. I just had to stay vigilant to avoid being attacked.

When he would look in my eyes and say, "I brought you into this world, I can take you out," I knew he meant it. He terrified me, but I was still hopeful somehow. I had a light inside of me that refused to be put out. I had a resilience that confused even me, but I learned to live without safety; to not even need it. Living this way became a theme in my life. I didn't know how to protect myself, and worse, I didn't think I deserved it. Growing up in a warzone became normal to me. Not having peace felt safer than having it. I was not allowed to have opinions that were different from my father's. My voice only mattered if it echoed his. I was not allowed to show emotion unless I was physically hurt. I was not allowed to have boundaries, and since boundaries are how you learn to love yourself,

I never learned to love myself. The bottom line was I began to believe that if my own parents had never been concerned with protecting me, why should I be concerned with protecting myself?

As I got older, my relationship with my sister never got better. My mother started treating her like her little friend by spoiling her, letting her have anything she wanted; probably because she was feeling the guilt of the divorce. Barely six months had gone by when my mom was set up on a date by our dear family friends. I encouraged her to go, because I knew she needed to move herself forward. That one date changed everything. The man who would become my stepfather saw the fragility and pain in my mother's eyes, and he stepped in like a hero. He was our knight in shining armor, and we were grateful. Things were moving really fast, but who was I to get in the way of this new opportunity for the life my mother always wanted?

My stepfather was older, sweeter, and had more class than my father. He was a gentleman, something I had not seen in real life. He spared no expense, spoiling us and making us feel loved and adored. Our first Christmas together was spent in Vermont, and he hired a limo to drive out all of our gifts. He gave my mom a five-carat diamond ring. Our lifestyle had suddenly gone from rags to riches...well they were pretty nice rags we'd been in, but this was a whole other level. I felt like I didn't have to pretend anymore. We were finally going to have a life I would be proud to show other people. It wasn't just going to look good on the outside, we were going to feel good on the inside too. I had always wondered what those happy families were really like, and now I had one! We even gained a step-sister and step-brother, and because they were so much older, they felt like an aunt and uncle. Everything was finally turning around!

I was glad to be off the hook for creating my family's happiness. I wasn't running the house anymore, but now my sister was. She was having night terrors, spending hours and hours in the therapist's office, and she

=

was afraid to sleep alone in her new room. I was just happy to be left alone to party with my high school friends. I was living unprotected and making adult decisions as a teenager. I couldn't figure out what was wrong with my sister. All our problems were over! It was like a joke to me. *I was the one who was verbally and physically abused and she's the one in therapy once a week? Did she end up on the floor being choked by our father when she spilled her milk? No. That was me. What a joke.* I knew she had probably witnessed some scary things, but they were never directed *at* her, so I couldn't understand why she was struggling so badly. I was resentful that she was seemingly sabotaging our new amazing life.

My mother was barely divorced when she married my stepfather. When I look back on how fast my mother met, married, and moved in with him, I realize there was no healing, there was no transition, there was no integration. We barely discussed what was happening, how it would happen, or what it all meant. No one asked me how I felt, and I never asked myself. Everyone just wanted to bypass the hard shit for a life that looked better on paper than it felt in reality. This abrupt change set me up for a lifetime of paving over the sinkholes, not asking what caused those sinkholes to form, and just moving on for the sake of survival.

My sister was in therapy once a week, and at one point her therapist asked to meet with me and my mom so she could understand all the pieces of my sister's trauma. When I mentioned the fact that I had taken care of my family when my dad left, my mom nearly got whiplash, turning her head to me and saying, "That never happened!" It was one of the most cutting, hurtful moments of my life. It was one thing that I had to live through a ton of abuse, but it was another when my own mother took something I was weirdly proud of surviving, and denied it even happening. I was crushed, but I told the therapist the truth. Later, with my mom out of the room, the therapist complimented me on my "resilience." If resilience meant not having any emotion, pushing through, and not needing safety then yeah, sure, I was resilient. Little did that therapist know I was putting myself in danger all the time. My favorite thing to do in high school was drive home late at night on the windy dark roads and see how far I could make it with my eyes closed.

When my sister was a teenager that whole "friend" thing with my mother started to backfire. She started acting out and my mom had no control. My moms lack of boundaries with my sister, led to my sister becoming more and more verbally abusive. My sister did as she pleased without fear of my mother's wishy-washy consequences. Like me, my mom never felt safe to have boundaries, my father had made sure of that. My sister could run her like a personal assistant all while she was disobeying all the rules. My sister wanted a place to put all her rage, and my mom was an easy target. My mom wanted to be liked more than she wanted to be a parent. With my father gone, the discipline went with him. My new step-father tried to warn my mom, even step in a bit, but my mom didn't listen. She would get defensive of my sister and herself. I tried to warn her too, and tell her that my sister was getting too out of control, and my mom knew it; sometimes she would ask for my advice. Once again I was the one directing and leading. I was sick of helping everyone, and never having the space to talk about my life and what I needed.

The fighting between my sister and I was increasing by the day. The truth was my sister and I were both desperately vying to be seen, heard, and loved. She would say to me, "Stop trying to steal all the attention!" I found this ironic because I thought the same thing about her. Attention seemed to be in very short supply. This made me hesitate before I told any story or joke around her. I would constantly shift myself into whatever she needed from me. It made me hate my personality, a personality I really loved until I was in my late teens. I would feel guilty for getting any attention at all, and yet I craved it. My sister and I would mostly fight for my mother's attention, the only difference was my sister chose every self-destructive and

=

aggressive way to do it. Our dramatic fights, the love-hate relationship my sister and I had, was now the new normal. It eventually became expected that at every family gathering my sister and I would have an explosive fight. Because of this, I was happy to be heading off to college, but little did I know I'd be taking my trauma with me.

I began looking for all the love my father hadn't given me in the arms of college boyfriends. I was desperate to be seen, loved, and validated. At first I tried to control all the relationships the way my father had, but slowly over time I became my mother; I was constantly needing attention, and staying in relationships that were degrading and unhealthy. My long term relationship with my college boyfriend was where I began to act out all the relationship drama I witnessed growing up including the fighting, the threats, the ultimatums, and getting back together after toxic fights. All the while, the real problem was my unresolved feelings for my father.

My journals from my college days are littered with rantings about my boyfriend and my father. I was living in Washington, D.C. one summer during college, and working there, but going to see my boyfriend in Pennsylvania every single weekend. I was terrified if he didn't call me every night. I felt worried, insecure, and panicked that he would break up with me at any moment. The PTSD of my childhood was manifesting as the hypervigilant girlfriend. The experiences with my college boyfriend directly mirrored my experiences of continued rejection by my father.

June 20, 1990

Did I tell you I called my dad the other day? Yeah. He was such a jerk. I made him a card, with pictures and a poem and sent him a present. He didn't mention any of it. I had to bring it up. I called his work number to wish him a Happy Father's Day, but no answer. I have to tell you I was pretty worried. Well, it turns out he changed his work number. Nice of him to tell me, huh? He spent Father's Day with his new girlfriend's family. He even took her to see Grandma, when I haven't seen her in 5 years. Then he complains to me that I never see her! Telling me how bad of a granddaughter I am? Whose fault is that? He rushed off the phone not caring what I had to say. Nice Father, huh?

My father couldn't spank me anymore, but he could ignore me, make me feel small, and use his new weapon; character assassination. Meanwhile my college boyfriend and I were on the same racetrack going in circles.

July 8, 1990

Today I called Craig after work and spoke to him for a while. He said he'd call when he got home from the bars but it's 1:07 AM and I doubt he'll call. I hate that because I wake up with the most horrible feeling that he's found someone else he'd rather be with.

This was almost every journal entry over the summer. Waiting for the calls, relieved when he did call and terrified when he didn't.

July 9, 1990

I called my Dad yesterday and he hadn't returned my call. Then he called with a new home number? Nice of him to tell me. He has moved in with his girlfriend, again thanks for telling me! I can't believe he's ignoring me again. I can never count on him at all. He always lets me down. I hate it. My dad is all about pleasing himself. That's what he does best. He has never considered the feelings of others or the consequences of his actions. I'm angry and upset and I feel like crying. If he's ignoring me now, imagine what will happen if he gets married? It makes me sick that I can't depend on my own father. My family will be so different. We will be a team, always helping our children and each other and giving support. I hope I don't end up marrying someone like my father.

=

A month later my father called my stepfather and mom's house and asked to borrow five-thousand dollars because his business was failing. He claimed he was suicidal. My mom said no. Imagine getting this phone call from a man that tortured you financially, emotionally, and physically. My stepfather was pissed. I was disgusted and sad. I felt abandoned and insignificant, so I tried harder to gain attention from boyfriends. Like my father, I demanded total loyalty and lots of attention. I continued to act out my relationship with my father with every man I dated well into my late twenties. I couldn't see the pattern and trauma I had been through. My sister and I were also acting out all the trauma we experienced growing up, and eventually it would lead to the end of us.

In many families, trauma isn't always recognized as trauma, it becomes the air we breathe, the water we swim in, so deeply ingrained in our daily reality that we don't even see it. Like the old parable of two fish swimming along, where one asks, "How's the water?" and the other responds, "What's water?"- we don't question what we've always known. When dysfunction, criticism, neglect, or even silence becomes the norm, we stop recognizing it as toxic; it's just life. We adapt, contort, and survive within it, never realizing that what we've internalized as normal is actually shaping our nervous system, our relationships, and our self-worth. Mid-life reinvention requires us to finally step outside the water, to look back with new eyes, question what we once accepted, and reclaim the parts of ourselves that were lost in the depths. Healing isn't about blaming or staying stuck in the past; **it's about recognizing what was, so we can consciously choose what will be.**

As we go through life, we pick up trauma like big rocks that we put in our jacket pockets. Pretty soon we are walking around with a heavy jacket full of rocks, feeling weighed down and not fully understanding why because we have become conditioned to the weight of it all. In my case, by the time I hit mid-life, I had a closet full of fancy jackets, and they were all full of rocks. These rocks we carry are the old wounds, unhealed relation-ships, outdated beliefs, and guilt that was never ours to carry, and the jacket I wore with the rocks from my sister became too heavy to carry an-ymore. We drag these rock-filled jackets through life, convincing ourselves that if we let go, we'll lose something. We have come to believe that if we drop a single rock, we'll be bad daughters, bad mothers, and bad people. We believe that if we take off the jacket, if the weight is gone, we will start unraveling and never stop. But here's the truth: It was never ours to carry. Some relationships, some beliefs, some stories, they belong to the past, not the future. But when you finally take that jacket off, you don't just lose the burden...you gain yourself. So tell me...what's in your jacket pockets? And are you finally ready to take the jacket off?

Visualization Exercise: The Rocks You've Been Carrying

Close your eyes for a moment and imagine this: You're standing at the edge of a long road, ready to step into your future. But you're wearing a jacket filled with rocks, and it's so heavy you can't take even one step. You can no longer stand up straight, and you see another rock in front of you, so you pick it up out of habit, because you always do.

Now, picture yourself trying to walk down that road. With every step, the jacket gets heavier. The weight pulls on your shoulders, your arms ache, your pace slows. Inside that jacket is everything you've been carrying for years; beliefs, past wounds, unprocessed trauma, and the echoes of things people said to you that made you feel small.

Think of the voices that told you: You're not enough. You can't trust yourself. You have to keep everyone else happy first. You should be grate-ful for what you have, why want more? You'll never be as successful, or as happy, and free as "those" people.

Maybe you don't even remember picking up these rocks, these limiting beliefs. They were handed to you by your parents, teachers, old relationships, and by a world that told you who you should be before you even had a chance to decide. "Here," they said, "hold this."

But here's the thing: That jacket? It's not yours anymore. You get to choose what you carry forward. And you can take that heavy, outdated jacket off. Right now.

The Power of Reframing

There's a Japanese art form called Kintsugi, where broken pottery is repaired with gold, making it even more valuable, beautiful and stronger than before. I believe the same is true for us. Your past is not a chain around your neck. It's not a list of failures. It's not proof that you're broken. It's raw material. It's the diamonds of your wisdom and growth. The moments you thought would destroy you? They're where your diamonds are buried. The times you felt abandoned? They taught you how to stand on your own. The heartbreaks you've endured? They showed you what you truly deserve. The failures you have survived? They refined you, making you wiser, sharper, and more resilient.

So what were the diamonds I found? My sister taught me how to have boundaries and love myself. My father showed me how to deal with trauma and helped me learn how to re-parent myself. My mother taught me that I didn't have to live a life sentence of trauma, I could free myself.

Here's the secret no one tells you: Your past is not happening to you; it's happening for you. So the question is: Are you willing to sift through the ashes and claim the diamonds? I know you're capable, you just have to be willing to show up for yourself.

Understanding the Subconscious Mind – The Hidden Operating System

Part of reframing and creating sustainable growth is accessing your subconscious mind. This is how I help my clients move through the pain and access their freedom. Here's something wild: Ninety-five percent of what you think, feel, and do is driven by your subconscious mind, which is the part of you that runs on autopilot. It's the part that was programmed before you even knew it was happening.

Think of your brain like a computer. When you were young, the "software" was installed; beliefs about yourself, love, success, and what's possible for you. The problem? Most of us never update the system. We're running our adult lives on outdated programming from childhood.

That's why you keep hitting the same patterns, feeling the same trauma, even when you consciously want something different. The subconscious mind doesn't care about logic, it only cares about keeping you safe based on what it knows. But here's the good news: You can reprogram it.

If you've ever felt stuck, like no matter how much you try to "think positively," your old fears, patterns, or doubts creep back in, it's because true transformation and healing happens beneath the surface. Pain has to be addressed from the subconscious mind. There are incredible methods I have used in my own life and with my clients that address this.

Healing Methods to Start Rewiring the Mind

- Rapid Transformational Therapy (RTT): A powerful method that combines hypnotherapy, neuro-linguistic programming (NLP), and cognitive behavioral therapy to create lasting shifts in just one session.
- Emotional Freedom Technique (EFT): Also called tapping, this method helps release trapped emotions and calm the nervous system through acupressure points.

=

- Breathwork: Using your breath to access parts of yourself and see what you need for deep healing.

These are just a few ways to access your subconscious. Your brain is always capable of rewiring itself. These methods help it rewire faster. Emotional healing also lowers stress hormones, like cortisol, which impact weight gain, anxiety, and disease. Releasing stored trauma helps shift your body from fight-or-flight to peace and safety, improving the overall health of the nervous system. This is why women who heal their subconscious mind suddenly find themselves thriving, in relationships, business, and health. Because when the brain stops running on the same old fears and patterns, it's so much easier to build something new. Letting go isn't just a mindset shift. It's life-saving work.

Guided Reflection: Finding Your Diamonds

Take a deep breath and think back to one moment in your past that still shapes your decisions today. Maybe it's a moment when you felt rejected, or a time you were told you weren't enough. It needs to be a failure that truly impacted you.

Now, grab your journal again and ask yourself:

- What story have I attached to that moment?
- Is it really true? Or is it just what I believed at the time?
- How has this moment actually prepared me for my next level?
- What's the diamond of wisdom in this experience?

The moment you rewrite the story, you change the outcome. Because your past does not define you. You do. And today? You get to choose a new narrative.

The Road Ahead – Lighter, Freer, and Ready

You started this chapter wearing a heavy jacket, weighed down by all the rocks you've picked up along the way. Now, you've set it down. You've uncovered the diamonds in your past. You've learned how to start rewiring your mind and body. You've taken the first step toward real healing. So, now? You walk forward lighter, freer, and more powerful than ever. Because the woman who is becoming limitless doesn't cling to the past. She rises from it. She uses her past as proof of her power. And that's exactly what you're doing.

As you've looked back on your past, you've begun to see the invisible weight you've been carrying; old patterns, inherited beliefs, and silent agreements you never consciously made. You've uncovered where you've given too much, settled for too little, and absorbed expectations that were never truly yours. Awareness is the first step, but transformation requires action. Now comes the moment where you decide what no longer belongs to you, and what you refuse to carry forward. **This is where boundaries come in.** Boundaries are not walls; they are the edges of self-respect, the lines that define what you will and will not allow in this next chapter of your life. If you are truly ready to reinvent yourself, boundaries are not just important, they are *essential*. Because the truth is, you cannot build a new life while still staying tethered to everything that broke you.

Chapter 3
Reclaiming Your Power – Boundaries for the Win!

"Sisters, sisters, there were never such devoted sisters. Never had to have a chaperone, no sir. I'm here to keep my eye on her. Caring, sharing, every little thing that we are wearing. When a certain gentleman arrived from Rome, she wore the dress and I stayed home."

- ROSEMARY CLOONEY AND VERA-ELLEN, "WHITE CHRISTMAS"

If you're feeling exhausted and overwhelmed by constant demands; pulled in a thousand directions by your family, your coworkers, your partner, or your inbox, your boundaries need to be stronger. If you're running on empty or struggling to feel joy in the things you used to love, whether that's your work, your relationship, or even time with your kids, your boundaries need to be stronger. If you feel numb, disconnected, easily irritated, and like you're constantly one step away from losing it...you've got it, you need stronger boundaries. In fact, there's a good chance your boundaries are not just unclear or not strong enough...they're nonexistent. And here's the truth: **Weak boundaries create a life that doesn't feel like your own.** And when your life doesn't feel like yours, it slowly starts to drain you from the inside out. Want to reclaim your energy, your clarity, your peace? Start by reclaiming your boundaries. Because without them, even the best parts of life start to feel heavy.

I know, because there was a time when I had practically zero boundaries for myself, my family, or other people. I was mad as hell about how people were treating me; annoyed that they were constantly disregarding my feelings. I also hated how I was reacting. I was resentful about how tired I was and how little time I had for myself. For some reason I didn't do anything to change it. Maybe I wasn't sure how. Or maybe it was because I would constantly tell myself, "Well, if I didn't do it, who would?!" Whether it's at home, or at work, or with yourself, a lack of boundaries leads to burnout. And burnout is now recognized by the World Health Organization as a syndrome. It's a thing! Having healthy boundaries means:

- You don't compromise your values to make other people feel comfortable or to be liked.
- You say no when you want to.
- You only offer what you're comfortable giving.
- You don't tolerate toxic behavior.
- You don't do things just because you feel guilty.
- You don't put yourself in unhealthy situations.
- You recognize that you are the only one responsible for your own happiness.

Boundaries are more important than you even realize. It's your personal code of conduct, grounded in your beliefs, morals and values. Boundaries are an invisible forcefield around your sanity. Boundaries help keep people, situations, and things away from you that steal your joy. Boundaries show people how much you respect and love yourself because boundaries are love; love for yourself, and for the people you're setting the boundary with. Boundaries will always be accepted and respected in healthy relationships, and they act as filters for the relationships that aren't meant for you.

Boundaries are really important for our well being, and the only reason we don't have them is because of fear. In hindsight, I can see so clearly how fear was controlling me. Fear of not being liked. Fear of letting my friends, kids, and co-workers figure things out on their own. Fear of using my voice and commanding respect. Fear I would get fired, that my kids would fail, or that my husband would mess everything up unless I micromanaged him. A funny thing happens when you start setting and enforcing a new boundary, and I know because I saw the shifts in my own life. When you start creating healthy boundaries, some people become very upset. The truth is that the very people who will become enraged and alarmed over your new boundaries are the very people who were benefiting from you not having them. You have been doing their spiritual growth homework and they have gotten used to that! They've gotten really comfortable letting you do all the heavy lifting, and not hearing you say, "No, I am not comfortable with that," or "This is too much."

You don't have to over-explain or justify your boundary to anyone. You don't have to accuse or blame the other person. You're taking responsibility for yourself and feeling good in your life. You don't need to apologize for your boundaries either. It's okay to disappoint people sometimes. It's okay to have peace, space, and time for yourself, and your own happiness, despite the chaos of other people's lives. I learned the tough lesson that you don't help someone who's fallen down into a well by getting down in there with them. You stay on the ground above and invite them to climb out, guiding them to use their own skills and resources without draining yours. Some will...and some won't. And that's hard. The truth is everyone is on their own divine journey, learning lessons that are specifically designed for them. Boundaries ensure that they get the lesson. Setting a boundary is not a one and done thing. You have to hold the boundary, even if it's hard. Mid-life is the perfect time to redefine your boundaries, and to ask yourself:

=

- What do I keep saying yes to that I don't want to?
- What am I really afraid of?
- Which people are energy vampires in my life and how do I lessen their impact on me?
- How can I create more time and space to do the things I really love?
- Where do I feel disrespected?
- Where do I feel depleted?
- Where can I bring more ease and calm into my life?

Use your journal and create some boundary mantras to keep you on track. The mind loves repetition so these will help guide you. Mantras like:

- I am not responsible for other people.
- I am not responsible for how people react to my boundaries.
- Boundaries are how I love and respect myself. Boundaries are love.
- Boundaries are always needed but in mid-life, they are your ticket to freedom.
- I'm not responsible for other people's happiness and success.

I learned about boundaries, or rather not having boundaries, early on. Growing up in an abusive household, I learned that boundaries were either nonexistent or dangerous. I was taught, through words, actions, or silence, that my needs, emotions, and personal space were irrelevant or punishable. I learned to shrink myself, ignore my own discomfort, and to prioritize keeping the peace over protecting myself. My survival depended on reading the room, anticipating others' emotions, and sacrificing my own boundaries to avoid conflict or harm. And now with my father barely in my life, I was still trying to set boundaries with my sister, but I had no idea what I was doing.

My relationship with my sister was becoming more like psychological warfare the older we both got. Keeping up with the chess game of trying to anticipate her next move was exhausting. Even as we moved further into adulthood, the drama never stopped. It was as if the old wounds we carried were not old at all. We could get back to those feelings of unworthiness, rage, and resentment in seconds when we were around each other. My sister found more and more ways to get the attention she wanted as a child, no matter the cost. She would rage at everyone in the family or destroy herself with addiction. Rehabilitation programs, therapeutic boarding school, therapists...nothing seemed to work. She was like a tornado that was taking everything down in her path. This began when my mother remarried, and got increasingly worse year over year.

Every holiday and vacation was a battlezone, a chance for both of us to get the attention of our new, blended family, usually by getting into a screaming match. I was only fifteen when my mom got married again, but I swore on my Laura Ashley bridesmaid dress that this was the beginning of the perfect family I had been dreaming of. We had money, a fresh start in a new house, and my mom was finally being treated with love and respect. My step-brother and sister were older, already out of the house, and seemed friendly, welcoming, and fun. They were happy that their widowed father found love again, and I was just happy for a do over.

But as time went on, they got to see the real us; the fighting, the screaming, and the volatility. Things began to shift, and we became a package deal gone wrong, a burden to everyone, especially my stepfather. My mother told us to straighten up, to be grateful for my stepfather taking us in and caring for us; we were lucky to be getting anything at all. This became her mantra and reason for everything. She would constantly tell us, "Be grateful! He doesn't deserve this stress. We're lucky to have him." I started to feel like damaged goods, worthless and unworthy of love. I learned that love was conditional because it would be constantly held over my head. It started to become clear that there was a divide between my stepfather's children and us. They were fun, honorable, successful, and we

=

were dead weight. This made our fighting even more intense because we started to see what we were fighting for. Love, attention, validation, and worthiness...all the things that were dwindling down to nothing.

Things got even worse between my sister and I after I graduated from college. Even though we were seeing and speaking to each other less and less, my sister began to explode over the most insignificant, mundane things when we were together. Like my father, she would go off like a grenade. Things like who could bring a boyfriend to Thanksgiving, what bedroom we got to stay in during our beach trips, or who was telling too many stories at dinner would enrage her. In her mind, she was always being neglected, given the worst, and considered the least. She didn't feel seen when I was around.

She didn't care about anyone else's needs because she didn't have the capacity for that, something I can recognize now with hindsight but had no way of comprehending when we were growing up. You can't pour from an empty cup, and her cup had been bone dry for years. It was all take and no give, and she was relentless in getting what she wanted. My family would always give in to her. She scared them to death. Any time I tried to assert myself, or defend someone else in the family, there would be a verbal attack thrown at me. This constant emotional cage match was brutal and my family would just stand by and watch. "We" were always the problem, which made the divide between my step-sister, step-brother and us even greater in my stepfather's eyes. After all, his kids were perfect. The more my sister verbally attacked me, just like my father had, the more the family backed off. Once again, I felt like I had no one protecting me.

I tried to fight for myself, but I was no match for my sister. She would usually take things to a level I wasn't willing to go. It would become borderline physical, and there was a guarantee for horrible insults and verbal abuse. She would literally scream in my face and then, just like a psychological thriller, convince my family I had caused it all. A lot of these attacks would start or end with a sinister smile at me across the dinner table. I was unable to read her body language to tell what would happen next. I felt unsafe and unable to protect myself because I'd never learned how, and no one wanted to intervene.

Occasionally my new family would try to break up our fights, but their way of handling it was to say things like, "You girls better stop this," and "You both need to get it together," which always made me feel misunderstood. I rarely instigated the conflict, but I would escalate it to try and stop from being abused. My mom and new family weren't interested in defending or protecting me, they wanted "us" to stop. The reality was my sister was now the abuser in the house. She was great at exploding with anger, shocking everyone into silence, and scaring the shit out of me. I can remember always feeling like, if only people knew what our family was really like. Turns out our family still looked good on the outside but not on the inside. Maybe nothing had really changed after all. I was becoming more and more depressed and hopeless.

Despite the chaos, despite the years of hurt, I always held onto a toxic level of hope for my relationship with my sister. That's what people don't always understand about abusive relationships, hope is the glue and the drug that keeps you stuck. No matter how bad it got, I believed that maybe the next time would be different, and that maybe if I just tried harder, loved more, and stayed quiet when I needed to, or said exactly the right thing, I could fix it. I longed for the kind of sisterhood I saw in movies, especially *White Christmas*. Every December, I would watch Rosemary Clooney and Vera-Ellen sing, "Sisters, sisters, never were there such devoted sisters," and feel an ache deep in my chest. I wanted that. I wanted a sister who loved me unconditionally; who would protect me, laugh with me, and always have my back. I wanted a sister I could trust, but the sister I had was nothing like that.

=

In my twenties, and with our relationship in the hope phase, I had invited my sister to Los Angeles to visit with me and stay in my apartment. At this point I was excited about my acting career and the class I was taking. There was a guy in my class I had a major crush on, but was too scared to talk to. I told my sister about it, probably because I wanted her to know he was off limits, but when I introduced them, sparks flew. I told him to not go near my sister, she was too young for him anyway. I told my sister to not go near him, he was known as a serious ladies man. They went home together that night. I was stunned and more depressed than ever. She even stayed over at his place. Part of me was worried sick, and the other part of me wanted to kill her. I started to think that maybe I was the crazy one. After all, she was the one he wanted. When she came home the next morning instead of remorse, she was full of entitlement. "He told me you guys weren't dating, what's your problem?" Her question cut deep.

What was my problem? The problem was for my entire life, nothing felt like it was ever mine. Everything was shared with my sister. My emotions, my anger, the abuse, my mother, and father, and the men I liked. This was the first time this happened, but it wouldn't be the last. My relationship with my sister was like a seesaw. I always hated seesaws because someone was always either slamming you into the ground or holding you hostage at the top. That's how our relationship felt.

Even with all of this, I spent years fantasizing about the kind of sisterhood I saw in movies; the deep, unbreakable bonds shared between women who grew up together. I wanted a sister who, even if we fought, would have my back no matter what. In my mind, I was Jo March in *Little Women*, scribbling away, working on my novel (except mine was a screenplay), while my sister rallied around me, reading my words with admiration instead of criticism. I pictured myself in *Practical Magic*, dancing barefoot in the kitchen with my witchy sister, drinking margaritas at midnight instead of dodging emotional landmines. And don't even get me started on *A League of Their Own* - I wanted that Kit and Dottie energy, where we could throw a few elbows, dramatically storm off to play for another baseball team, but ultimately tearfully hug it out at the Hall of Fame induction.

Instead, my reality felt more like a psychological thriller, where I was never quite sure if I was getting the fun-loving sister or the monster in the plot twist. I kept thinking if I just believed in it hard enough, I could manifest a movie-worthy relationship. But life isn't scripted, and no amount of *White Christmas* singalongs or Hallmark-level optimism could rewrite the role my sister was determined to play. Believe me, I tried.

Our relationship was a cycle of laughter, connection, cruelty, and abandonment. She could make me laugh my ass off and feel like we had the most unbreakable bond, and then, in an instant, she could turn, and I would realize I was with a psychopath. We'd be doubled over with laughter, lost in our shared history, reminiscing about childhood adventures, and for that brief moment, I would let myself believe...I would tell myself, *This is it, we've finally turned a corner.* But it never lasted.

The shift would always come, sudden and sharp, like a trap door opening beneath me. All it took was a look, a phrase, or a shift in tone, and I knew I was about to fall. The cruel words, the manipulation, the rejection...it would all start again, leaving me gasping for air, wondering what I had done wrong this time. We were always competing. We were like two leading actresses vying for the same part. It was always about who was the cutest, funniest sister; all that mattered was who had it all together. She never wanted it to be me, and I never wanted it to be her. When she wasn't going to be in the same space as me, I felt like I could breathe. Family vacations were better, and holidays were less stressful. She probably felt the same way about me too, and yet we were longing for sisterhood in our own ways.

I can remember at the age of eight years old going away to sleep away camp in upstate New York. I was crying hysterically when I left, afraid to leave my volatile home. It was all I knew, and I had no idea what was ahead of me. It was an all girls camp and my first real experience of sisterhood. Around the campfire every night we would sing heartfelt songs, arms around each other's shoulders, holding hands, hugging; I'd never felt so safe in all my life. I had never been offered this level of affection and closeness. It brought tears to my eyes. We had "big sisters" who were older campers that would look out for us. We laughed, played games, and went to chapel together. I can remember never wanting to leave, and sure enough I cried hysterically again, this time because I knew what I was really coming home to.

Going to college was transformative for me in so many ways. For the first time I had the space and feeling that something was truly mine. College was my experience and no one else's. I could reinvent myself as a more powerful, confident version of myself. I got to be the woman who would never take this treatment from her sister and family.

It was in college that I experienced my second moment of sisterhood, when I joined Kappa Alpha Theta. These women had no idea how starved I was for a sister. I was encouraged, supported, and loved like never before. I gained confidence and became a leader, holding jobs, throwing events, and mentoring the younger sisters as they joined. I started seeing myself as my own woman, separate from my family. I started to gain a deeper appreciation for how my stepfather had stepped in when my father abandoned me. My father stopped paying for college after the first year, and my stepfather started paying so I could stay.

In my time after college I moved to New York and started improv, as well as stand up and acting classes. I was focused on getting an agent right away and auditioning. It was validating to be good at something, and to be recognized. Acting classes felt like a deep healing. They showed me where I was wounded and I started to see myself as a woman who could change herself. I started delving into personal growth work and reading books on trauma.

When I moved to Los Angeles and began screenwriting, I sold my first screenplay right away. I was creatively reborn without my sister around. I wrote a song and sold it, started booking commercials, and I started creating the life I really wanted. The one area that was not improving was my relationships with men. Those were still filled with pain and suffering and I couldn't figure out why. I was longing for connection and love, but didn't know how to get it or keep it.

After a slew of dead-end relationships, my roommate invited me to her boss's son's two-year birthday party in the Hollywood Hills. She swore it would be fun and more adults than kids, which I doubted. I can remember walking into that party swearing off men all together. I said to myself, *Maybe I don't need to get married. I'll have a kid for sure, but I don't need a man in my life. I'll be happier on my own.*

I walked into that party and soon began a conversation with my now husband, Brett. I was drawn to him because he was wearing a white Lacoste shirt, khaki shorts, and docksiders; my dad's weekend uniform. We started chatting and laughing and he gave me his card. I thought nothing of it because I had sworn off men! A week later I invited him to a party celebrating selling my first screenplay. I barely spoke to him, but a week later he invited me to dinner. When I walked into the Fairmont Hotel in Santa Monica, I was scanning the lobby for him. When I caught sight of him he was smiling at me from ear to ear. I said, out loud and involuntarily, "I'm going to marry this man." He moved in with me two weeks later.

Right around this time, September 11th, 2001 happened. It was enough to burst our love haze bubble, and yet it didn't. My dear friend Michelle lost her husband that day, like so many others. Brett agreed to accompany me to the funeral in New York. One problem...he was going to meet my sister. At this point we only saw each other for holidays and family events, but I felt like I needed to warn him. I didn't know how to tell him, and truthfully, all our stories seemed embarrassing and shameful.

=

The funny thing is I thought they said more about me than my sister. I tried to tread lightly, and started with, "My sister and I have never gotten along." It was a massive understatement.

When she met us at Grand Central Station, I didn't recognize her and it scared me. She was dressed more elegantly, she had matured, and she had altered her face. Her lips were huge and so were her cheeks. She looked like a different person. I tried to act normal. That night at dinner I tearfully told Brett everything. I was fairly sure he would end things right then and there. *Who would want to deal with this?* He hugged me and told me he was sorry about how I was being treated. I was shocked that he didn't minimize it all or try to make excuses for her like everyone else had my entire life. With Brett, I had finally started to break away from my sister.

And yet, I always went back. That's the thing about dysfunctional relationships, you keep returning to the place that wounds you because you are chasing the moments that heal you. I convinced myself that if I could endure the bad with my sister, I could somehow earn the good. But the good was never real, not in the way I desperately needed it to be. It was a mirage, just close enough to keep me reaching, but never solid enough to hold. I wanted my sister to be someone she couldn't be, and I sacrificed parts of myself trying to make it so. This went on for years and years. We would be on these gorgeous family trips to Hawaii, Florida, Lake Arrowhead, the Dominican Republic, even on safari in Africa, and she would find a way to attack me and terrify everyone else during every single one of them.

When I met my husband, I finally had confirmation and validation about what I was living with. At the age of 32, I finally felt seen. And even more, he came to my defense. My family could deny the truth, but Brett saw it and called it out. At first I tried to minimize and hide how bad things had gotten, and of course when he first experienced being around her, she was on her best behavior, playing the part of the loving little sister. But soon, her anger and rage came to the surface, and Brett saw firsthand how fast the switch could flip in my sister. He also saw that his seemingly independent, strong girlfriend had no boundaries or self-esteem. He could see that when I was around my family I was a different person. I was back to feeling desperate, being performative, and dancing as fast as I could to avoid the landmines.

My sister would hurl an insult across the table, a knife dropping moment, and the look on his face said it all. *What the fuck?* I had kept this part of my life a secret from everyone, because I thought no one would believe me and because I was filled with shame. Sure, my friends knew I didn't "get along" with my sister, but they didn't know that she called me a "cunt" across the dinner table in front of my young nieces and nephews, or that she slept with one of my highschool boyfriends, or that she would try to physically fight me over what bed she got to sleep in at our Florida house. Brett hadn't seen that yet, but he would see as time went by.

My husband's love for me, his wanting for me to have boundaries, made me start to feel brave enough to have them. After we were engaged, Brett joined a family vacation we took to the Dominican Republic. At that point he'd been doing a great job at running interference. He had realized if my sister couldn't get me alone, she couldn't attack me as easily. He noticed how she would wait for me to walk away and then follow me. So he went everywhere with me. We were a united front against the tornado, and to my surprise, it was working. But one night, after a few drinks, I went to the restroom alone during a dinner out, and she cornered me in the bathroom.

"Brett's something else," she sneered at me, "you know he doesn't fit into our family right? He's not cute or funny...seriously Liz, what are you thinking?" She was in my face now, with these whirly eyes, like a crazy person.

"Well good," I snapped back, "because I'm going to marry him, not you." I gave her a coy smile and turned on my heels to go back to the table. This was the first time I was brave enough to stand up for myself on this level. Brett could see right away that something had happened, but I gave him a look that said "I got this."

That first boundary setting was a victory. Standing up to her, standing in my power, felt incredible and simultaneously frightening. Telling her I was going to marry Brett regardless of her opinion felt like I pulled the trigger on a grenade. One thing was for sure, I never wanted to be alone with her again. With Brett by my side I felt powerful. After that bathroom confrontation my sister tried to win Brett over, but he knew who she was. He was adept at playing the role of sweetheart fiancé, fantastic brother-in-law, but in reality he was head of my security, something I had never had before. I was letting him in more and more, and so, once we had been dating for a few months, I felt safe enough to take a trip to see my father.

The most complicated families are the ones woven together with pain and longing. My relationship with my father had evolved into a new phase, where I had become the doting daughter. He was an abuser, and left us practically penniless after the divorce, and yet, I still craved his love. That's the seductive nature of abusive relationships; even when they hurt you, they keep you coming back, chasing the approval that always seems just out of reach. I believed the story he told the people. He was a successful, retired businessman who played the stock market, had traveled the world doing exciting business deals, had royal English lineage, and a strong family line in the South. He was a magical storyteller, and I wanted to live in that story.

With him, I felt a strange and unshakable pull, a belief that if I could just be good enough, successful enough, impressive enough, he would finally see me, and maybe finally be proud. In some ways, I felt closer to him than my mother; in my mind he was the strong one, the successful one, the one who had boundaries. My mother was broken, weakened and weary from all that had happened, but he stood tall, even if his strength came at the cost of everyone around him. I mistook his distance for power and his rigidness for certainty, believing that if I could somehow get inside the fortress of his love, I would finally feel safe. But the tragedy of loving someone like that is that the door never truly opens, and you spend your life knocking, waiting for an invitation that never comes.

With my new head of security in tow we had many great visits with my father. Brett was enamored with him, mainly because I didn't tell him how abusive he used to be. I wanted to have some of my family feel as good as it looked. My husband's family didn't have the money and success my family had, but they had something my family would never have...trust. They could trust each other and be vulnerable. In my family, I had to dodge and weave and walk on eggshells.

My father sat at the head of every table, and he ran each one like he was helming a battleship. He was commanding, charismatic, and everyone did as he said. Because of this, at every restaurant he would order a slew of appetizers that most of us didn't need or want but ate anyway. Sometimes he would even tell us what to order for our entrees so that he could have a bite of everyone's food. It was all part of the show so we played our parts. On one of these occasions, I wanted to order eggplant parmesan and my father said to order a pasta dish instead. Brett spoke up and said I should order what I wanted. It was a record scratching moment, and my father was pissed. I even remember back tracking, saying it was okay and I wanted the pasta anyway, but Brett saw how afraid I was, how domineering my father was, and he understood that he needed to help me build some stronger boundaries.

On our annual visit to Florida for Thanksgiving, I was newly pregnant with my first child at the age of thirty-six after a long battle with infertility. The in-vitro had worked and everyone was excited. Well, almost everyone. My sister was angry as usual, not just because she was relegated to a hotel because of lack of space, but because I was getting attention. I was tired of walking on eggshells so when she confronted me about the unfairness of

=

not getting to stay in the house, I told her to back off and went to take a shower. I tried to calm my nerves; my head of security was with me, I was going to be a mother, all was well. I let the hot water wash down over my head, and my newly pregnant stomach. Suddenly my sister barged into the bathroom and pulled the shower door open. I started yelling for her to get out, but it didn't matter. She started screaming and yelling at me. I felt emotionally and physically vulnerable, obviously, because I was naked. I got out of the shower, trying to back her out of the bathroom, grabbed a towel to put around myself, and screamed at her to get out. As Brett arrived, she shoved me, and I almost fell over. Brett grabbed her and took her out of the room before locking the door.

This was the first time my sister had gotten really physical with me. It brought me back to all of those times I was defenseless with my father. I cried on Brett's shoulder, shaking in my towel. I cried for that scared little girl I was and for me now. My sister denied what had happened, and my family didn't want to make it worse so they didn't press the issue. Brett and I set bigger boundaries around how much we would see her, increased the security, and awaited our son to be born. Looking back I feel bad for Brett, walking with me onto the battlefield of my life, but in reality he was saving me from myself. He was giving me the courage for what was to come.

I remember the final months when my sister and I were in contact. It was 2019, I was forty-nine years old, and we were trying to make this sister thing work for the millionth time. Our final fight seems petty looking back at it, but after decades of conflict that led to me feeling sick to my stomach and hopeless about connecting with my sister, it was the final straw. Ironically, we were now both married, both had kids, and our lives had finally come together. On the surface our relationship had a real chance. My kids got along with her daughter and step-kids, and our husbands did, too. We were starting to try and trust each other, find common ground, and forgive. We made a pact to remain calm with each other, assume the best of each other, and tell the truth, but deep down I didn't trust her; too much had happened, and I remembered the seesaw. I still felt the weight of her demands and control even though they now had a softer touch.

What hadn't changed was that my sister would be offended and upset at the smallest things. Even when I would make an effort to repair things, she would turn it into another lesson for me. In her never ending "how to be a better sister to me" manual, I could never measure up. I took a family picture for her, and posted it on Instagram with a loving caption. She asked me to take it down because there was a cement wall behind her in her garden. I tried to reassure her that no one would even see or pay attention to that, and that she looked great. She was not having it.

"You actually love to take ugly pictures of me," she said in response. "You don't even know you're doing it, but I know you do it on purpose." *How can I not know I am doing something while also doing it on purpose?* I was so confused, but I said nothing. I took the picture down and accepted what she said. Once again, the rules of the game were changing, I had to stay alert and vigilant. I was a pro at walking on eggshells, so I would keep doing it around her, just like I did around my father, but deep down I was growing very tired of our dysfunctional relationship. The years had taken their toll on my mind, body and spirit. I was starting to feel like I couldn't do it anymore. Like I was physically unable to walk on the eggshells anymore. And every time my phone buzzed early in the morning with a text that said, "Can you talk?" my stomach would drop.

My stomach was betraying me more and more, saying all of the things I couldn't. I was in distress and it sounded the alarm, even when I wasn't around my sister. These stomach issues went on for years, and no doctor could solve it or diagnose it. It had started with my college boyfriend Craig and it had gotten worse over time. But every time a text or call would come through from my sister, I knew what was coming...another lecture about what I had done wrong and how to be a better sister. I had violated a new invisible rule, and it would either turn into a brutal fight or a demand I couldn't say no to. No matter how many boundaries I wanted or tried to create, it felt like I was always losing ground. She could come at me anytime, and I would let her.

I told myself countless times that it was enough. It was time to end the relationship with my sister for good. For years, I knew the truth. I knew that it would never work, but I was too scared. I had already lost so much. My father's love was conditional, my mother's attention was split, my childhood home never felt safe. And even though my sister and I had a relationship built on eggshells, screaming matches, and exhaustion, I couldn't let go of what little family I had left, so I stayed in it a little longer.

An abuser doesn't always raise their voice or their hand, sometimes they break you in silence. They are masters of manipulation, weaving control so seamlessly into the fabric of your life that you don't even realize you're tangled in it until you try to move. They don't have to scream to be terrifying, and they don't have to hit you to make you feel small. Instead, they demand total loyalty, not through love, but through a carefully constructed system of fear, guilt, and obligation. My father and sister didn't need to lash out physically or emotionally anymore, because their power came from something deeper; a constant, unspoken rule that to stay close to them, I had to abandon myself. Their love was a transaction, and the price was my identity. They could rewrite history, twist the truth, and make me question my own memories, all while making me feel like I was the problem, the difficult one, the one who needed fixing. And when I pulled away, the punishment was quiet but brutal; exile, withdrawal, a slow, deliberate erasing of my place in their world. It wasn't about anger, it was about dominance. Their loyalty test was simple: You're either with me completely, or you're against me, but what they never counted on was me finally choosing myself.

For years I dreaded every holiday with my sister, every family gathering, every interaction. I would be trying to come up with plans and strategies to keep her happy, desperate to create peace and love between us, all the while having debilitating stomach aches. Weeks before I knew I was going to see her, I would become physically ill. My body was screaming at me, "Don't do this. We don't want this. Please." I ignored it over and over again. But one last brutal battle between us went too far. And to be honest, because healing doesn't happen without honesty, I started that last fight.

Maybe I knew it was the only way to make myself wake up, stop walking on eggshells, and be done forever. It started with a mundane moment on the phone with my mom. I was complaining to her that my sister had left a crib at our family beach house, and the crib was taking up the whole guest bedroom where I slept. My mom got riled up and phoned my sister, and before I knew it, my phone was ringing. I picked it up, thinking naively that we had grown past these big fights. My sister started screaming at me; she was enraged on a level I had never heard before. Her tone was more brutal and more alarming than I'd heard before. And this time, she crossed the line and went for my kids.

She tried to put them in the middle of our fight, accusing them of being in on what was happening. When she started describing my kids as villains, making up stories about how they were giving her "looks," and needed to be better to her, something clicked. They were innocent. They even liked my sister, they were not going to be put in the middle of this. She was not going to do to them what she had done to me. The generational change was starting now. It was going to stop with me. I may not have known how to protect myself from her before, but I knew how to protect my kids. It was over. I would disconnect from her. There would be no more contact. This was the end of it.

For years, I had let my sister manipulate, control, and intimidate me. I told myself it wasn't that bad. I convinced myself that if I just worked harder, if I was more understanding, more patient, less sensitive, I could make our relationship work. I ignored the gut feelings, the red flags, and the emotional whiplash of never knowing whether I was about to be embraced, attacked, or discarded. **I betrayed myself over and over again for the illusion of peace.** Because that's what happens in toxic relationships. I had learned to tolerate, to adjust, and to endure. I told myself it was easier to stay than to face the consequences of walking away. But then, I finally did it. I set the boundary. And what I felt wasn't guilt, or devastation, or even anger. I felt *relieved*. It was a quiet, unexpected relief, like taking a deep breath after holding it for too long. I'd been holding my breath practically since birth without realizing it. It was like stepping out of a room I hadn't even realized I was trapped in. For the first time in years, I didn't have to brace myself for the next blow, the next seismic shift, or the next betrayal disguised as love. I didn't have to keep playing a game where the rules changed without warning. I was *free*.

But the fear still lingered. Letting go wasn't easy. *What if I was wrong? What if I was being too harsh, too unforgiving?* The self-doubt still plagued me. The fear of walking away from someone who was supposed to love me felt almost as heavy as the years of pain I had endured. Because the truth is, cutting ties with an abuser, even an emotional one, doesn't just mean losing them. **It means losing the version of yourself that kept hoping, kept trying, and kept believing they would change.** And that was the hardest part. Because if I wasn't the person constantly trying to fix this relationship, then who was I? If I wasn't fighting for her love, where would I place all that energy? The answer came slowly, in the stillness that followed the breaking point. I would place it in *me*...in *my* healing, in *my* future, and the life I was finally choosing to build for *myself*. And that's when I knew I was never going back.

My mother tried to accept this new normal, but at the same time couldn't let herself believe it was permanent. Like many times before, she thought this was just a break, but when she and my sister started to plan a Palm Springs Thanksgiving trip, and she tried to include me, I once again held the boundary. It hurt my feelings that my mom was choosing her at that moment, but I knew I had to choose myself and my family. At this point my step-sister and step-brother were doing their own trips and leaving my sister and I out of it. I don't blame them. They were sick of the toxic dance, but when I told them I was no longer going to have her in my life they acted like it was nothing. They still text us both to this day, not remembering that my sister's number is permanently blocked in my phone. I get texts saying, "I love that! Great picture!" But there is no picture for me. There is also no part of me that wants to see anything she's sending. The decision I made all those years ago still feels good in my mind and body, even today.

Setting the final boundary with my sister was terrifying. The moment I did it, a wave of regret, doubt, and confusion crashed over me, all just different names for fear. *Had I done the right thing?* I asked myself that question I don't even know how many times. It felt unnatural to protect myself, like I was breaking some unspoken rule I had followed my entire life. But this time, I had no choice. I had to protect my children, and to do that, I had to protect myself. For the first time in a long time, I chose me. I chose love, because boundaries are love. I imagined myself saying to my sister, "I love myself so much that I have to end this relationship." I chose my well-being over my extended family. I had chosen my peace over having a sister. And even though it felt unfamiliar, even though my hands shook, I stood my ground. It was uncomfortable. Having boundaries felt so wrong and so foreign that I questioned myself at every turn. I tried to shrink the truth of what had happened, gaslighting myself into believing I was exaggerating, that it wasn't that bad, just like I always had. I caught myself second-guessing, wondering if I was being too dramatic, if I should just let it go, smooth it over, keep the peace like I'd always done. And then I looked at my children's faces.

No. I couldn't go back. They wouldn't grow up in the same toxic patterns I did. If choosing myself meant losing everything, so be it, because in the end, I *finally* had myself. And when the fire burned everything down, I found all the diamonds in the ashes.

The Diamonds

I started to trust myself, my voice, and my choices. I started to put myself first and care for myself in a way I never had before. Mentally and physically I poured into myself and healed. My mother and I redefined our relationship. We got closer and learned to trust each other more. I leaned on my sisters-in-law who became my real sisters. I can remember sitting at the dining room table, afraid to really let my sister go. I had tears in my eyes, knowing I was going to block her permanently on my phone, afraid of retaliation. I was realizing I would never have a sister again. "We'll be your sisters!", they said. We hugged and cried and sealed the deal. Rachel and Marie have been the diamonds in my life ever since. I accepted their unconditional love and felt the peace I had always wanted. With my new found strength and loving support, I started a podcast, then a business, and then a movement. All because I felt safe. I started living in safety and protection with loving boundaries.

If you're going to reinvent yourself, **boundaries are non-negotiable**. They are the foundation of your transformation. Reinvention isn't just about changing careers, relationships, or routines; it's about redefining how you allow yourself to be treated and how you honor your own needs. Without boundaries, you will keep pouring your energy into everyone else's expectations, leaving nothing for your own growth, healing, and expansion. Reinvention requires space, mental, emotional, and physical, to become the next version of yourself, and that space is only created when you stop overcommitting, over-explaining, and over-functioning. You cannot step into the life you desire while still saying "yes" to what drains you. **The woman you are becoming doesn't tolerate what the old you settled for.** Boundaries are the doorway to your future self, and if you're serious about reinvention, you must guard that door fiercely.

Boundaries are the invisible lines that define what we will and won't accept in our lives, yet so many women reach mid-life realizing they've never truly had them. Instead, they've been conditioned to be accommodating, agreeable, and available to everyone but themselves. Women have been conditioned to believe that sacrificing is honorable, without realizing it's stealing our souls.

A lack of boundaries isn't just about saying "yes" too often, it's about self-abandonment, it's about believing that other people's comfort is more important than your own needs, your own peace, and your own joy. The truth is, boundaries are not selfish; they are a radical act of self-love. They teach others how to treat us, showing them what we will and will not allow. They create space for healing by breaking patterns of over-giving, over-explaining, and over-efforting. Boundaries are the declaration that **you matter, your energy matters, and you are no longer available for relationships, commitments, or obligations that deplete you.**

For many women, the struggle with boundaries is rooted in trauma. If you grew up in an environment where love was conditional, where your needs were dismissed, or where you were expected to anticipate and manage other people's emotions, then saying "no" as an adult can feel unnatural; even dangerous. You may have learned that people-pleasing equals safety, that avoiding conflict keeps the peace, or that your worth is tied to how much you do for others. But the cost of a life without boundaries is high. You will take on all of the resentment, exhaustion, anger, and you have to live with the nagging feeling that you're being taken for granted. Not to mention the stress it puts on your body.

People-pleasing isn't a personality trait, and it's not you being "nice." It's a trauma response called "Fawning". It's what happens when you learn at a young age that being agreeable, likable, and low-maintenance keeps you safe. Maybe love was conditional in your home. Maybe anger wasn't allowed. Maybe the only way to belong was to abandon yourself. So you became the chameleon. The fixer. The good girl. You scanned every room for emotional temperature, adjusted your tone, shrank your needs, and called it kindness. But underneath the compliance was fear; the fear of rejection, conflict, or being "too much." Healing means recognizing that the version of you who learned to please was simply trying to survive. And now? **You get to choose something different.** You get to speak, take up space, and stop apologizing for existing.

If you constantly feel depleted, if you replay conversations in your head wishing you had spoken up, if you say "yes" when every fiber of your being wants to say "no," then your body is waving a red flag that you are living without boundaries. Healing starts the moment you stop betraying yourself to keep others comfortable. The moment you realize that your needs are not burdens, they are your birthright, massive shifts begin to happen. Here are some common boundaries you can start setting right now to start feeling those shifts. This list comes from my own experiences as well as many of my clients:

- If you have children, start trying to give them a little more independence, especially in problem-solving situations. For example, if your teenager sends you a text about something that doesn't involve you, encourage them to try and work it out themselves before you step in. It's okay to not have all the answers all the time.

- Start saying no to social events you don't want to attend. Not having any interest in being there is reason enough, you don't have to make up excuses. It's either a hell no, or a hell yes.
- Practice not attending family events when you know they feel uncomfortable or exhausting to you.
- Leave those after-hours work calls and emails unanswered; they will still be there when the next business day begins.
- Just because other events are on the calendar doesn't mean you can't take time for yourself, even in small ways. Start carving out space in your schedule regularly for alone time.
- If you are married or in a relationship, consider taking a trip by yourself and exploring some new places. You will learn so much about yourself.
- Practice changing plans as needed without taking on the guilt you have been conditioned to feel when doing so. It's okay to back out of plans, even if the reason is simply because you have changed your mind and don't want to be there.

Really what all of these boundaries boil down to is one point: You are not "on call" for everyone else's emotional moments. Your boundaries will help the people you care about to grow. They are an invitation to their own progress. Instead of dropping everything and abandoning your needs, the next time someone you care about is in need of something, ask them, "What do you want to do about this?" Tell them you are confident they will make the right choice. Empower them. Don't take on the responsibility of their emotional or physical well-being; you can better serve them by taking care of yourself first, and showing up for them only when you have the capacity to meet them where they're at.

External boundaries like how you spend your time, saying no to chairing the fundraiser at your kid's school or your favorite charity for example, allows someone who needs some leadership experience to step up. Internal boundaries can look like not checking your work emails on the weekend, so that you can live in spaciousness and ease. If you know that checking your email or texts compulsively gives you stress, set a boundary with yourself.

I wish I had realized sooner that boundaries were the only way to free myself. I wish I could shout this from the rooftops so that every woman could know that this is a huge part of the new era of mid-life. This is part of the legacy we need to live now so that we can show our daughters that they can be free to choose a life they love. It's the way you show that little girl who is still within you that you are protecting and loving her. You are giving her what she has been longing for.

And yes, setting boundaries can feel uncomfortable, scary and awkward at first. But you know what's worse? Living a life you don't recognize, like, or want...a life where you don't own yourself and your choices.

Exercise: Your Boundary Blueprint

Find a quiet space, take a few deep breaths, and place your hand over your heart. Say to yourself: "I give myself permission to protect my peace. I am worthy of ease, clarity, and joy."

Now grab your journal and answer the following:

Part 1: The Boundary Audit

- Take an honest inventory. Where are the leaks in your energy?
- Where am I saying yes when I really want to say no?
- Who in my life consistently drains me, and what boundary have I been avoiding with them?
- What obligations do I resent, but continue out of guilt, fear, or habit?

- Where in my life am I over-giving, over-functioning, or over-explaining?
- Where am I not honoring the boundaries I have tried to set with myself?

This is a friendly reminder to be radically honest with yourself; this isn't about judgment, it's about clarity.

Part 2: Create Your "Hell Yes & Let Go" List

Make two columns:

HELL YES: List the people, experiences, and values that give you energy, peace, and purpose.

LET GO: List the things that deplete you, keep you stuck, or pull you out of alignment with your truth.

Draw a big line between them. This is your new boundary line.

Part 3: Boundary Declaration

Fill in the blank and speak these phrases out loud:

- I am no longer available for _____.
- I choose to protect my time, energy, and peace.
- I am not here to be liked, I am here to be aligned.
- Boundaries are not walls, they are the bridges to my freedom.

Exercise: Embodiment Practice

Write, read, and say your new boundary mantra: **Boundaries are how I love myself. Boundaries are how I free myself. I am allowed to protect my peace.**

I challenge you, with love, to take one action that reinforces this in the next seven days. This is the work of reclamation. You are not "too much" for wanting peace. You are not "selfish" for wanting space. You are simply waking up to the truth. You are coming to really understand that you don't owe anyone access to you just because they're used to having it.

Boundaries aren't about pushing people away. They're about pulling yourself closer. You're doing the brave work now. *Keep going.* Boundaries aren't optional at this stage of life. They are your ticket to peace and happiness. Setting boundaries isn't just about protecting your time or saying no; it's about honoring who you are now, not who you used to be. When we draw that line in the sand, we're not only reclaiming our present; we're signaling to ourselves that we're ready to stop living from old wounds and outdated roles, and that means looking back. Not to stay stuck in the past, but to understand the stories we've been telling ourselves, and rewrite the ones that no longer serve us. Because the next chapter isn't about repeating what's been; it's about consciously creating what's next.

Chapter 4

Reframing the Past and Writing Your New Story

"Don't be afraid, I can meet you halfway. We can't always know where the road ends up, but with some luck I know we can go wherever we imagine. Why should we wait? Later on may be too late. 'Cause where can we run when you see there's half a chance that we might really become whatever we imagine?"

- JAMES INGRAM

The quote I chose for this chapter was the one I chose for my senior quote in my yearbook. It still brings tears to my eyes. I always wanted to believe I could have a life of whatever I imagined, and have a partner to share it with. After all the work I have done on myself, that's exactly what I have in Brett. He's the most open hearted, expansive, deep thinking man on the planet. And he's a great storyteller, so am I. But unlike my father I don't use my stories to perform anymore, I use them to gain perspective. One thing I've learned that has changed my life is that I am the author of my life and stories. And like any good storyteller, I have the power to edit, rewrite, and reframe the way I see my past. And the most beautiful part of this realization was learning that every single woman has the power to do this for herself, too.

For too long, many of us have carried the weight of old narratives, stories that paint us as victims, that keep us small, that tell us life happened to us instead of for us. But here's the truth: Once you become aware of how your past has shaped you, you get to decide what it means. You get to choose whether your experiences are a source of pain or a source of power. You are just *that* powerful.

So far in this book, I've walked you through my awakening, where I realized something wasn't quite right, kind of like waking up and realizing I had been wearing shoes two sizes too small for the past twenty years. Then, I moved you into the awareness phase, where I bravely dissected all the reasons I had been stuck, exhausted, and maybe even a little resentful. And because you are so powerful and brave, I know you have started to recognize these things in your own life, too. You've started to face the hard truths, unlearn some outdated survival tactics, and possibly wanted to throw this book across the room more than once. Good. That means it's working.

I've shown you what it looks and feels like to start finding diamonds in the ashes of life. Hopefully you have started to see the lessons and wisdom you've gained. And I got really honest with you about where I needed to have better boundaries. I hope it encourages you to look at where you need more boundaries in your life. Now you know that boundaries are not selfish, they are self-love, and that you have the power to shift your future using boundaries. We're ready now to start stepping into The Reframe; the part where you get to flip the script. This is where we stop seeing ourselves as extras in someone else's movie and start taking the lead role in our own lives. This is where we take all the tough moments, the heartbreaks, and the disappointments, and turn them into the origin story of our power. Healing is about awareness, but true freedom comes from reframing, from reclaiming your past as a foundation for the person you are becoming.

Reframing is not about denial. This is not a toxic positivity bypass where we start sugarcoating and using my least favorite "F word," *fine*. It's not about pretending that painful things didn't happen. It's about looking at what did happen and choosing to see the wisdom, the strength, and the transformation that came from it. It's about refusing to stay stuck in the same, tired narrative of suffering, and instead finding the diamonds buried in the ashes. Healing is about awareness, but true freedom comes from reframing; from reclaiming your past as a foundation for the woman you're becoming. And trust me, she is *amazing*.

One of the first steps in reframing your past is noticing the patterns that got you to where you are today. Recognizing generational patterns in our families is a vital step in reframing the past, not to assign blame, but to understand. When we begin to look at the stories, behaviors, and coping mechanisms passed down through generations, we gain clarity about what shaped us. But this work requires neutrality. You're not here to relive old wounds, you're here to witness them with compassion so you can decide what no longer belongs to you. This kind of observation creates space for post-traumatic wisdom; the kind that says, "It may have started with them, but it ends with me." By acknowledging what's been inherited, you give yourself permission to release what you're ready to let go of, and consciously choose what gets carried forward. That's how legacies change.

In writing this book I have had many revelations. I am a mindset teacher, a transformation coach, a healer, and guide, but even healers need more healing. Teachers need guidance, and coaches need to keep growing, learning and expanding. And so I did. I wanted to take an even deeper look at the patterns of my past and see what else I needed to let go of, forgive myself for, and reframe.

I started to see the stories of my past differently as I was revisiting them. I started to see my mother's, sister's, and father's experiences with neutrality and through a more compassionate lens. I started to see their

=

point of view and the similarities in my own life. I had unknowingly done the very thing I swore I would never do. I carried patterns from my upbringing into my parenting. Some of these past traumas and wounds I addressed before I became a mother, but there were other more subtle, more insidious patterns that now, looking back, I can see clearly. To get to this point of understanding and compassion, I had to drop any judgment of my parents and sister that I was still carrying. Where there is judgment, there is no learning. You can't be curious and judgmental, and I wanted to see what had yet to be uncovered.

My father had a hard childhood, cut short by an abusive and domineering father. He passed that down to me, but looking back I saw how my father felt trapped in his role as a father. He was depressed and resentful. He was a performative storyteller in public, but mostly miserable at home. He craved excitement, depth, meaning, and purpose. I can remember him leaving enormous tips for waitresses in small towns and sneaking out before they knew it was him. I can remember him buying groceries for an older woman ahead of him in line at the grocery store who didn't have enough money. And I can remember the stories he would tell about himself. He would tell me about being made to buy his own clothes starting at ten years old, and about how he got all D's in high school, but got into college. He told me how he bought himself a purple Jaguar, how he got himself into Wharton Business school, and how he was eventually hired to a top firm on Wall Street.

As the story went, my father was invited to the palatial home of his potential new boss at the firm. They went hunting on his property, and took a Jeep out early in the morning. As they drove along, he asked my father about his childhood, and how he got into Wharton. Soon they came to a creek that a tree had fallen across. The road was impassable.

"Looks like we'll have to head back," his potential boss said, and started to back up. According to my father, he stopped him, jumped out, gathered all his strength, and moved the log so the Jeep could cross.

"I've taken three other guys who wanted this position out here and they all accepted what I told them and we went back to the house," he explained once my dad was back in the Jeep. "You're the only one who got out and moved that log. You're the only one who was willing to find the solution. You're hired." My father was a bootstrapper, a dreamer, and had a generous, kind heart. He wanted more, just like I did. Just like me, he didn't think he could be a parent and have all the things he really wanted.

My mother was the oldest child, and the one who was expected to know better, even though she was completely unprepared. She was attending an all-girls college when she met my father. When she got pregnant with me her whole life changed. She felt trapped and scared to be a mother. She figured she made her bed so that was that. She wanted to live the life of an artist with creative freedom, but that was not possible anymore now that she was thrust into the reality of adulthood. She threw herself into volunteer work, later becoming the president of the Junior League in our city. I can remember meetings in my home, watching her shine and lead. She was an art teacher for high school kids at the private school where I attended as a kindergartner. I watched how those kids adored my mother and valued her opinions. She was encouraging and a masterful guide. She was coaching, loving people, and leading, just like I do now. She wanted to feel like what she was doing made a difference. She wanted to leave an impact on the world. When she married my stepfather she was finally free to do all the things she always dreamed of, but she still felt stuck. Her children were struggling, and she wasn't sure how to live her dreams and keep us safe. She never dealt with her trauma, she was too busy trying to help my sister. She wasn't sure her dreams mattered, or that she was worthy enough, to have them. She felt the weight of self-judgment for the choices she had made in the past and couldn't forgive herself.

My sister was born into a chaotic family of survivors. She watched my father scare us and control us and she tried for a time to be the joyful, lighthearted one, but that role was taken by me. She needed attention and love, so she became the rebel, the outward indicator of all of the things hiding beneath the surface. She couldn't and wouldn't pretend she wasn't hurt, traumatized, and terrified, like we did. She wanted someone to take responsibility for what had happened, but no one would. Her rage was covering the deepest sadness. Her lashing out was a way to get the attention she so desperately needed. She wanted to be loved by her family, but we were too busy surviving. She, like me, wanted a sister, a loving father, and a present mother.

My sister is funny...not just funny, but hilarious. She uses humor in her parenting, as a way to connect with people, and to heal, just like me. She's determined to parent her daughter differently, and to give her everything she didn't have. She wants to break the generational pattern. I hope she will. Patterns are tricky because until you see them, you'll keep repeating them. Until you know what you want to leave behind you can't make generational change. Until you see the diamonds in the ashes, you can't see your legacy. Until you stop blaming everyone and everything for your behavior, you can't change it. This is how you gain post-traumatic wisdom. Post-traumatic wisdom is the deeper knowing that emerges when we choose to face our pain, not with fear, but with the intention to grow. It's the diamonds we mine from our hardest experiences that hold the truth we can carry with us once the shock, survival, and shame begin to settle. It doesn't mean the trauma disappears or that what happened was "meant to be." It means you've decided that what happened doesn't get to define you; it gets to inform you. **You are smarter, wiser, and more powerful than your past.**

When I began to see the patterns, how my mother silenced herself, how my father coped through control, how my family avoided feelings and emotions, I started to awaken. I could see the threads and patterns of how my life was woven together, and in seeing them I gained the power to *break them*. This is where healing meets evolution. I no longer react from old wounds, I respond from new awareness. I stopped reliving my past and began *rewriting* it into a story that supports who I was, and still am, becoming. It's not about erasing the past. It's about rising with it and using it as the foundation for a new, more empowered future. Without even realizing it, you have been building a foundation of diamonds. I imagine myself, and the new life I'm building, while standing on the diamonds of wisdom. My post-traumatic wisdom has been exponential in doing this work over the years with myself, with my clients, and even more with myself in writing this book.

One part of my life where my post-traumatic wisdom shows up the most is with my son, Landon. I want to show you how I found the diamonds in the ashes of his birth story and created a new foundation and a new story about my life. In doing this, it not only changed my story, but it changed Landon's as well.

One thing I never saw coming was that I would have trouble getting pregnant. After all, I had been on birth control since I was seventeen, trying desperately *not* to get pregnant. It felt like a terrible joke. Infertility brought my husband and I to our knees. We wanted a baby so badly. After battling through infertility, enduring in vitro, and finally getting pregnant, I naively believed that all my troubles were behind me. *I had done the hard part, right?* I had fought for this child, endured the rollercoaster of trying to conceive, and now, I was going to have my happy ending, dammit!

In the final weeks of my pregnancy, I had a feeling something wasn't right. He was a big baby, but I noticed he wasn't moving enough. Thank God for my maternal instinct, because it saved his life. Women's intuition

=

is not only real, it's something we must rely on, lean on, and learn to trust. More on that later…

I went to my doctor, and even though she checked me I still felt something wasn't right. She tried to reassure me, but I could not, and would not, be reassured. She sent me to the perinatologist for a deeper look. At this point I was addicted to watching two TV shows on TLC; *A Wedding Story*, and *A Baby Story*. I was basically a professional wedding planner and an obstetrician by that point. When the doctor performed an amniocentesis, a procedure where they test the amniotic fluid for abnormalities, the liquid he pulled out didn't look right. Somewhere in my mind a check engine light went off.

"Is everything okay?" The urgency and worry in my voice was obvious.

"Yes, everything is okay, but out of an abundance of precaution let's just induce you today." He was trying to sound calm and casual, but my gut was screaming at me. *Something is wrong.* I'm sure he could see the concern and doubt all over my face.

"If there was a problem, we'd have that baby out in twenty minutes," he said in his most reassuring voice. *But I'm a doctor now,* I thought, *I've seen this play out on TV a million times. Something is wrong…*

As my husband and I walked over to labor and delivery I started to doubt my intuition. *Maybe I was making this whole thing up, maybe I was just being paranoid! I'm a first time mom, not a doctor.* When we checked in with the nurse, all of my doubts came pouring out of me.

"I think I'm losing my mind," I said, as she started taking my vitals. "My mom isn't here, I don't have any of my things…maybe I should just go home and wait to have this baby." Just as I was beginning to believe my doubts over my intuition, a new nurse walked into the room.

"Honey, that baby is coming out in twenty minutes," she said. *Great,* I thought, *I'm fucked.* Before I knew it, I was being prepped for an emergency C-section; I was thirty-six weeks pregnant. The epidural wasn't working, his heart rate was dropping, and they were struggling to get him out. They even had to vacuum him out of my stomach because his shoulders were so big. And then, after he was out, the thing every mother dreads most—silence. No cry. No sound.

They whisked him away to the NICU with my husband trailing behind, and I laid on the operating table, staring at the ceiling, tears slipping down the sides of my face as they sewed me up. I had waited for this moment for years, and had worked so hard to get it through fertility treatments, but it turned into a nightmare in the blink of an eye. I have never felt more alone, more terrified, and more helpless in my life. Landon was born with right arterial thrombosis, a collection of blood clots in his right arm. He had suffered a stroke at birth. The doctors told us he could be brain damaged. They were unsure if his right arm would survive, and told us that if it was causing him too much distress, they might have to amputate it.

I was in my own personal hell, and of course my husband Brett was, too. He was going into work everyday, trying to hang onto his job and his sanity simultaneously. He would go to work all day while I stayed in the NICU, and then as soon as he was off of work, we would switch shifts and I would go home for a shower and some food. It was like walking away from a bad car accident and coming back to the scene each day. We were disoriented, confused, and moving slowly through all the phases of this new reality.

I wasn't allowed to see Landon the first few days of his life because I was sick with postpartum preeclampsia. My blood pressure was high and they couldn't wheel me into the NICU. My mother made the mistake, although she meant well, of showing me a video of him. All the tubes, buzzing monitors, him looking unconscious...I began to disassociate. I started to shut down. I left my body and started to deny this was happening to me. As I left the hospital days later without my baby, I ran

=

into an old friend. She was leaving the hospital with her newborn daughter, wrapped in a pink blanket, a picture of perfection. She asked about Landon, and I wanted to lie. I wanted to say, "Everything is fine," but the truth came out, and she looked at me with sympathetic eyes, which made me feel sick. I didn't want pity. I didn't want people looking at me like I was the mother of a tragedy. I was detaching more and more.

I was so afraid Landon would die that my mind began preparing for it. I started pretending he had never been born. It was easier that way. People reached out, offering love, support, and meals, but I didn't want to let anyone in. I was drowning in fear, in grief, and in the weight of the unknown. When I finally got to see Landon, five excruciating days later, something incredible happened. He opened his eyes. He looked at me, and then he looked at all the monitors and tubes, and then he looked back at me as if to say, "What is happening to me!?" I saw the fear in his little eyes. I realized this kid was not brain damaged, he knew everything that was happening! That day I made a decision. I was going to show up for him and bring him through this. I knew this would require me to step out of my past and rise into the kind of mother books were written about. I knew I needed to un-armor my heart. I knew I had to become a Warrior Woman. I had to show up for Landon with the heart, wisdom, and strength of a warrior so that he could make it through.

As I opened my heart, something else started shifting inside me. Friends kept showing up. The meals arrived, the calls continued, the prayers were offered, and slowly, I let them in. I realized I needed people. I couldn't do this alone. And then, the miraculous happened. Landon started getting better. He started to heal. He was doing so well that they gave him a brain scan to see if the damage had improved. I'll never forget the technician's face, especially because I thought something was wrong. I was so prepared for bad news.

"What's wrong?" I braced myself for impact.

"I can't find it," he said, and I was confused.

"Can't find what?"

"The damage to his brain," he said, "it's gone. There's nothing there." *A miracle,* I thought, *Landon is a true miracle.* His brain was healed and his arm was stable. After fifty-two days in the NICU, we were finally going home. I had prayed for this moment, dreamed of it, and now that it was here, I was terrified.

I was going home with a newborn whose right arm was bloody and scarred. *What kind of life would he have? Would people stare? Would they be scared of him? Would he always be seen as different?* I felt myself shrinking, staying small, and retreating into the safety of my house, where I could control who saw him, who judged him, and who pitied him. Close friends came over, their faces full of love, encouragement, and hope. They reassured me and reminded me that he was home. They encouraged me to love on him, and reminded me that was safe and so was I. He was going to be okay. I pushed through my fears and started taking him out publicly.

I dressed him in the most adorable little outfits like embroidered Jon-Jons with tiny frogs or cars. I dressed him in the preppiest baby clothes I could find. And yes, there were stares. At first, I ignored them. I braced myself for the comments, the questions, and the cruelty of the world. And then, it happened. A woman stared at us for what felt like forever. My heart pounded. I sat up straight, ready for battle. She walked over to our table, and I held my breath.

"I love that embroidered outfit! Where'd you get it? She is such a pretty baby!" *Wait... what?! She had no comment on his arm. She thought he was a girl!* I was floored. In that moment, I realized something profound: I couldn't control how people reacted to Landon. But I also didn't want to assume every interaction would be a negative one. From that day on, I made a decision. I wouldn't hide Landon's arm in long sleeves or jackets unless it was cold. I would stop assuming the worst in

=

people. I started taking him to mommy and me classes, to the park, and to lunches with friends. And you know what? Most people didn't say a word. They treated him like any other baby. And when they did ask, I learned to be patient, to give simple explanations, and to not carry the weight of other people's discomfort. Then, the next big step...preschool.

I felt like fear was going to swallow me alive. *Would kids make fun of him? Would they exclude him?* I walked him in, trying to keep my emotions in check, and watched as he joined a group of kids playing. A couple of kids looked at his arm. One even reached out and touched it. I held my breath. And then? They moved on. That was it. No drama. No cruelty. Just kids being kids. With tears in my eyes, I turned to his teacher and told her my fears. She smiled and said, "All parents feel this way. I find it's much more upsetting to them than it is to the kids."

I looked around at the other parents, all teary-eyed, and all terrified in their own way. We were all hoping our kids would be accepted. We were all letting go, trusting that they could handle this next important step toward independence. That's when I realized the real lesson: Landon wasn't just on *my* journey. He was on his own. I had spent so much time worrying, protecting, and fearing the future, but Landon? He was just living. He was happy, he was resilient, and he wasn't thinking about his arm the way I was. I had been projecting my fear onto him. The more I reframed this story, and the more I saw it as a miracle rather than a tragedy, the more I believed in his strength and his divine path. Landon was loved, guided, and supported by God, the Universe, and Spirit. His life wasn't something to grieve, it was something to celebrate. We started to celebrate his life in every way possible. We focused on what he could do, not what he couldn't. We found a ton of diamonds on the journey of raising a child with a different arm; a child who was a walking, talking, living, breathing miracle. And now? As I write this book in 2025, he's eighteen-years old and just got accepted to his first-choice college.

The fear I carried for years was wasted energy. Landon has always been whole. His journey was never about what he lacked. It was always about what he would overcome. The past is only as painful as the story we tell about it, and I refuse to tell a story of fear when this has always been a story of power. Landon's journey hasn't always been easy, but it has always been divine; divinely unique, divinely timed, and divinely orchestrated. Believing Landon is on his own divine journey is not a one and done thing, it's taken time to believe it and embody it. But when I did, I watched Landon do it too. That belief carried him through over fifty surgeries on his arm, including a bone lengthening surgery that went terribly wrong. It carried him through struggles with neurodivergency that meant going to three different high schools, struggles to find a solid friend group, heartbreak, and applying to colleges with a less-than-stellar grade point average.

We will never really know what happened the day that Landon was born, but since I rely on my intuition, I'll tell you what I feel happened. When Landon was born he had the cord wrapped around his neck four times. He was born with a fully developed arm, but it was turning blue and the skin was sloughed off. I think Landon felt the cord tightening around his neck, put his arm up to free himself, and got his arm stuck in the cord. Then he couldn't move which let me know there was something wrong. I noticed a stark difference, a drop in movement and kicks while he was in utero. So guess who saved Landon's life? Not the doctors, not me, but Landon himself. Landon saved his own life. He is the hero of his story and you are the hero of your story too.

The funny thing is people assumed Landon's birth story was a negative one, and that I would never try to have children again, but I had the power of reframing on my side, and decided to bring my beautiful second child into the world. I was all geared up to go for a second round of in vitro, but there was one problem, I wasn't getting my period! I was waiting and waiting until my mom suggested I take a pregnancy test.

=

"Mom! You know I can't have children without in vitro!" I was so offended by her suggestion.

"Just go pee on a stick," she insisted. I went off in a huff to the bathroom. Low and behold that pregnancy test revealed two, dark pink lines! I came out of the bathroom waiving my pregnancy test in the air as if it didn't have pee on it. We were overjoyed. What had happened to Landon was a lightning striking event, but my doctor took every precaution anyway. She watched my pregnancy even more closely, I went on a blood thinner, and I enjoyed my pregnancy. Doing so many ultrasounds and tests was fun because I was always getting updates. One day when the doctor called to tell me all the latest tests were normal, I noticed a little excitement in her tone.

"Do you want to know what you're having?"

"Of course I do," I said.

"It's a *girl*," she said, as she emphasized the word "girl" with a tone of power and prowess. I screamed with joy. I honestly felt like I won the lottery, and I did. Landon was two-years old and the cutest little blonde boy. I dressed him in a pink lacoste shirt and we drove up to Brett's job site. Landon handed Brett a card that said "It's a girl!" We hugged and cried. We felt overwhelmed with joy, and we have felt that way ever since. Coco brought a bright light into our home. She was a wish and a prayer and everything I wanted. But what if I had told myself a story that I was cursed after what happened to Landon? Or that I wasn't safe to roll the dice again? Coco restored our faith. She reminded us that, just like Barry Manilow sings, "We dreamers have our ways of facing rainy days, and somehow we survive." Coco is wise and intuitive. She's learning more about boundaries in her high school years. Only recently has she learned what happened with my sister. She has her own Warrior story, but I'll save that for the next book!

Reframing your story helps you heal the past and gain the confidence to change your future, but first you have to see the deeply held patterns and understand what you've been carrying all these years.

Exercise: "What Am I Carrying That Isn't Mine?"

This exercise is designed to help you uncover hidden beliefs, behaviors, and emotional patterns that may have been passed down to you or shaped by past experiences. These patterns often operate silently, but once you see them clearly, you can decide what to *release* and what to *reclaim*.

Take 15-20 minutes with your journal and reflect honestly. You are not judging the people in your life; you're becoming a conscious observer of the patterns that shaped you.

Step 1: Look Back

Answer the following prompts with curiosity and compassion:

- What messages did I receive growing up about:
  - Love
  - Success
  - Rest
  - Emotions
  - Boundaries
  - Money
  - Identity (who I was allowed to be)
- What did I learn about how women should behave in my family or culture?
- Who did I have to be in order to feel safe, accepted, or loved?
- What patterns do I see repeating in my family (generational behaviors, trauma responses, roles, silence, sacrifice)?

=

Step 2: Identify the Pattern

Circle or highlight any recurring themes you notice. These could be things like:

- "I have to earn love."
- "I must always stay strong for others."
- "It's unsafe to speak up."
- "I am responsible for everyone's happiness."

Write down the patterns that no longer serve you:

- What patterns am I ready to let go of?
- Which ones were never mine to carry in the first place?

Step 3: Reclaim the Truth

Now rewrite the narrative. For every limiting belief or pattern, write a new truth that supports who you are becoming.

For example:

Old Pattern: If I'm not doing everything for everyone, I'm unworthy.

New Truth: My worth is not measured by how much I give, my presence is enough.

Close with this reflection:

"I honor the past, but I am no longer ruled by it. I now choose beliefs and patterns that align with my healing, power, and future. I am the author now."

This is how legacy shifts, from one woman deciding: *It ends with me.*

Exercise: Rewriting the Story That's Been Running Your Life

Step 1: Name the Story

Think of a painful or defining experience from your past, something that still lingers in your thoughts, actions, or self-talk. It could be a childhood memory, a difficult relationship, a moment you felt powerless, or a traumatic event (like Landon's birth). Write out the story as you've always told it. Be honest. Don't hold back. Let the emotions, blame, guilt, and beliefs come through.

Step 2: Identify the Narrative

Ask yourself:

- What beliefs did I create from this experience?
- What did I make it mean about me? About others? About the world?
- How is this story still showing up in my life today?

Step 3: Find the Diamonds

Now, look deeper:

- What strengths did I build because of this?
- What did I survive, learn, or gain?
- What part of me became more powerful, more compassionate, or more intuitive?

Step 4: Reframe It

Take your pen and write the story again, but this time, from your higher self. Write it as the woman you are now; the one who sees meaning, power, and wisdom. This is your new story, and it is one rooted in resilience, not regret. It is one that claims your power instead of giving it away.

=

REFRAMING THE PAST AND WRITING YOUR NEW STORY

Guided Reflection

- What story have I been telling that no longer serves who I'm becoming?
- What's one belief I've carried from the past that I'm ready to release?
- What truth do I know now that I didn't know then?
- If I could speak to my past self in that moment, what would I say to her?

This exercise not only allows you to release old pain, it helps to alchemize it into purpose. We can reframe the past, but that doesn't mean fear disappears. It's still there, still lingering in the background, waiting to pull us back into old patterns. If we truly want to move past what happened to us, we have to go deeper. We have to call on the biggest super power we have. We have to call on the little girl inside of us. The truth is we never really grow up. That little girl is still there, waiting and hoping you'll come back for her. Let's go get her.

Chapter 5
Heal the Girl and the Warrior Will Appear

"Hey little girl, when you grow up don't make the same mistakes I did. Learn to say, 'No, I've had enough.' Then nothing and no one can hurt you. Follow your heart and you'll be fine. Follow your dreams and take all of the time that you need."

- MADONNA

There is a moment in every woman's life when she realizes that the strength she's been praised for might actually be armor. It's the smile that hides the pain. It's the productivity that masks the exhaustion. It's the caretaking that distracts from the emptiness. And beneath that armor is a little girl. A little girl who wanted to be seen, heard, protected, and loved. The truth is, the woman you're becoming—the powerful, expressed, joyful, lit-up version of you—can't fully rise until the girl inside you feels safe. That's what this chapter is about; doing the "little girl work." Because when you heal her, the warrior finally gets to rise.

My own little girl had a motto. "Be good, be funny, take care of everyone, and then they'll love you." She was the people-pleaser. The fixer. The golden child. The glue that held everything together. The girl who knew exactly how to act perfectly so no one would get upset. But she was also the one who didn't know how to feel safe to cry. Or scream. Or say, "That hurt me, don't do it again."

I had discovered this work over the years and reconnected with "Libba," the little girl version of me. I called myself Libba because I couldn't pronounce Elizabeth and it just stuck. When I think of her, I picture her with two long pigtails at about six-years old. There's a picture of me around this age dressed in a red turtleneck and red pants with a red and navy flowered headband. She has a knowing smile that I love. I can see how wise she was, even then.

For a long time, I thought I was successful at keeping Libba hidden and protected. The truth is, though, she was everywhere. She showed up in so many ways; in my relationships, in my marriage, in my parenting, in my friendships. She was the voice that said, "I'm tired, I need to rest. When is someone going to put me first!? Why does everyone leave me?" Meanwhile I shushed her. "Don't rock the boat," I said, even when I was drowning. I was orphaning her every time I ignored her pain. She was like a dog barking to be let inside, and I let her scream. She was too vulnerable, too needy, and too innocent. I was afraid to talk to her, and to hear what she really was thinking about me and my choices. I thought I was protecting her, but I was really protecting myself from her. I neglected her for years and told myself it was the only way to survive.

The turning point came while I was receiving a Rapid Transformational Therapy session. I met my six-year-old self on the floor of our old living room, holding her breath. She wasn't fine. She wasn't okay. She was terrified and exhausted from trying so hard to be good. She was exhausted from not knowing the ever changing rules. She was scared of the constant threats of violence. That day, I made her a promise. *I see you now. I'm not leaving you again.* Everything changed. I stopped performing. I stopped pretending. I started listening to what she needed. And when she felt safe, I felt free.

We all wear masks. But the cruelest ones are the ones we crafted in childhood. Not to deceive others, but to protect the little girl inside; the one who wasn't sure she was ever enough as she was. I was the pleaser, the server, and the perfect one. I was the woman who did it all and made it look effortless. I wore the mask of perfection like armor, believing that my worth depended on my achievements. My days were a blur of endless striving, but underneath the polished exterior, I felt empty. I was tired, numb, and constantly asking myself, *Why isn't this enough?*

It started early. I remember being eight, standing in the kitchen, holding up a drawing I'd spent hours perfecting. My mom glanced at it with distracted approval, but her attention was already pulled elsewhere. I asked her to hang it up on the fridge, and she paused. "Let's save the fridge for really special art," she said. In that moment, and many others, I began to believe that nothing I did was truly good enough. I learned that praise was earned, not freely given. *Do more. Be better. Maybe then she will see you.*

I wore the mask of the performer. I learned to perform to feel valuable, safe, and loved. I learned that love was conditional, reserved for moments of manipulation to get what you needed. I remember trying to show my love to my father and stepfather so that they would pay my college tuition. Everything had a price. Nothing was given for free. So, I worked harder to become better. I pushed myself to earn friendships, boyfriends, popularity; anything that would earn me that elusive approval. And it worked, or so I thought.

But there was a cost to ignoring the little girl. As I grew older, the stakes got higher. The pleasing of everyone became a full time job, but the emptiness echoed in my chest. I hustled, I performed, I pleased; yet, inside, I felt a constant ache. I had built my entire identity around striving for approval, but I had no idea who I was without the applause. I was disconnected from my little girl; the creative, joyful, expressive part of me that didn't need to earn love to be worthy of it. And as long as I ignored her, I

=

remained disconnected from my own joy, authenticity, and fulfillment. I wore the mask of the one who held it all together. I knew how to collect gold stars. I knew how to earn applause, admiration, and results. But I didn't know how to rest. I didn't know how to receive love without doing something to *deserve* it. I didn't know who I was underneath the mask, only that I was terrified to take it off.

My days were full of doing, fixing, producing, leading, but nights? Nights were full of doubt. Nights were filled with questions like, Why do I still feel so alone? When do I get to feel peace? But the little girl was locked away. I refused to listen to her. I stopped playing. I stopped dreaming. I stopped *feeling*. I was numb. And I had mistaken that numbness for strength. I thought being tired all the time meant I was important. I thought self-abandonment was sacrifice. I thought never asking for help made me powerful. But really, I had abandoned the part of me that made me feel *alive*. My little girl didn't care about perfection. She cared about joy. She cared about being seen.

She cared about creating just because it was fun, not because it was impressive. She didn't want to please anyone anymore. She wanted to be free. She didn't want to have to hold everything together anymore. She wanted to know she was loved for who she was. But I kept pushing through, doing more, and ignoring her. And the longer I ignored her, the more lost I became, until I had no idea who I was anymore. It remained this way until I turned forty-nine and said to myself, *Who is this person I've become? I don't know who this is. This shell of a person, this woman who's waking up in the middle of the night worrying, this woman who has high blood pressure, who's overweight, and drinking too much...this woman is not me!*

And so I let Libba in. I opened the door, unsure if she would even want to speak to me. At first she didn't trust me, but then our hearts couldn't help but reconnect. The moment I saw her in my mind's eye; small, scared, and clutching that old drawing that wasn't good enough for the fridge like it was her lifeline, I broke down. I realized how much I had abandoned her. I realized how much I had silenced her voice in my quest to be perfect. I held her, legs dangling down, tears on my shoulder. I was crying and letting her cry too. We were crying all the tears we hadn't been able to cry for decades.

I told her she was safe and that I'd never leave her ever again. I told her she was enough exactly as she was. I told her she didn't have to perform, please, or achieve to be loved. And as I spoke those words, I could feel something shift, a weight lifting. I could feel a softness returning. Reconnecting with my little girl allowed me to reclaim my emotions, to open my heart wider, and to trust in myself. It allowed for my creative expression, joy, and intuition to return. I no longer needed to hustle for approval or prove my worth. I could create from a place of alignment, not fear. The more I embraced her, the more powerful I became.

I spent years being the "good girl." The responsible one. The one who kept the peace, avoided conflict, and met everyone else's needs before her own. From the outside, I seemed generous, selfless, and endlessly accommodating, but inside, I was screaming. I was giving so much of myself away that I had nothing left. I was living for everyone else and slowly dying inside. I can remember my parents fighting by having explosive arguments that made my whole body shake. I remember hiding under my blankets, praying to God for silence and safety.

There were nights when it got so bad that I believed I could die. I believed that my father would kill me one day in a rage, and there would be nothing my mom could do to stop it. When morning came, I would be relieved. *I made it.* I would carefully move out of my stuffed animal barrier that I created around myself for protection and peek out of my bedroom door. *Silence, no one in the hallway, I'm safe.* Hearing the sounds of breakfast being made, I would tread down the stairs carefully, making sure to smile. *Be helpful. Be good. Make them laugh,* I would tell myself.

=

If I could just keep everything peaceful, I believed I could hold everything together. So I learned to shove down my own needs, my own emotions, and my own voice.

That pattern followed me into adulthood. I became the fixer, the pleaser, and the caretaker. My relationships were built on compromise and overgiving. I buried my own dreams because I believed it was selfish to put myself first. I couldn't hear my own voice anymore. I was disconnected from my intuition, from my desires, from my true self. I had silenced my little girl so completely that I couldn't even remember what she wanted.

I was working with a client who kept saying she felt invisible. She signed up for a "Warrior Soul Healing" Rapid Transformational Therapy session with me. As I guided her through her own healing process, something inside of her cracked open. I saw her little girl. She was quiet, obedient, and trying so desperately to be good enough to deserve love. I realized how deeply she had betrayed her. She had been sacrificing her own needs to make everyone else comfortable. I asked her little girl what she wanted, and for the first time in years, she spoke. She told Danielle she wanted to be seen, to be heard, and to be loved for who she truly was, not who she was pretending to be. The tears flowed, and she was reborn.

Just like Danielle, reconnecting with my little girl allowed me to reclaim my voice. I was finally able to set boundaries without guilt. I was free to create a life that was aligned with my desires, not everyone else's expectations. I learned that true strength wasn't about being "good" or "perfect," it was about being true to myself.

So many of the women I coach come to me saying, "I don't even know what I want anymore." They've lost their voice. Their identity. Their spark. What they really mean is that their inner child stopped feeling safe a long time ago, and they've been protecting her ever since. But protection eventually turns into suppression, and suppression becomes numbness. Reparenting yourself is the sacred act of giving yourself what you didn't receive as a child; nurturing, protection, emotional validation, and boundaries. It's how you break generational patterns and stop negotiating your worth. When we are children we expect that our parents will meet all our needs. When they do not, then we assume it's because of something we did. The mind starts to say, "I must be unlovable. I must not be good enough. I'm not worth it." We carry this into adulthood in subtle, and not so subtle, ways.

We look to our partners, friends, our job, and sometimes even our kids to meet these needs, not knowing we can meet those needs ourselves through this work. The truth is you have everything you need, but the little girl needs to know that you care enough to reconnect. There's a piece of us that still begs for space to be seen and heard. When it is healthy, we feel connected to its creativity, inspiration, and excitement. When it is wounded, we become disconnected from its energizing qualities and are left feeling deeply unhappy and resentful.

Recently I listened as my hairdresser complained about her husband. I've been going to her for years and she's seen me through many ups and downs. I listened as she told me she wanted her husband's attention, his love, and for him to put her first and care for her. I stopped her, tears in my eyes, and said, "Everything you're asking from him, you have to give yourself first." We hugged and cried. She was going through an identity theft issue, a job change, undiagnosed physical issues, and was now having anxiety attacks. She wasn't giving herself any care at all. She was pushing through and trying to outrun her emotions. "You have to release this emotion," I told her. "This is why you're feeling these physical symptoms and the anxiety attacks are happening."

When you finally turn inward and begin to heal your inner little girl, when you sit with her, listen to her, and love her, you begin to meet the needs that have gone unmet for far too long. You stop begging the world for scraps of love and start pouring it from your own overflowing cup.

=

You stop returning to the people who don't have the capacity to give you what you need, hoping they'll somehow be different this time. You stop going to the empty well for water. Because now you know: The love you were missing didn't vanish, it was buried. And you're the one who gets to unearth it. That's where the real freedom begins.

But know this: Healing and reparenting your inner child is a journey. It's not a one-time event, it's a sacred, ongoing evolution of healing. It's choosing, day by day, to return to the parts of you that were silenced, shamed, or forgotten. It's learning to listen to your own heart with the tenderness you always needed and never got. It's messy, nonlinear, and often uncomfortable, because you're not just healing memories, you're re-wiring beliefs. You're becoming the parent, protector, and provider your little girl always deserved. Some days you'll feel cracked open. Other days, wildly free. But every moment spent reconnecting with her brings you closer to wholeness. You don't have to do it perfectly. You just have to keep showing up; for her, and for you.

You're not just revisiting the past. You're reclaiming the parts of yourself that were left behind. You're rediscovering the parts that are still holding the keys to your joy, creativity, truth, and power. When you reparent yourself, you stop waiting for someone else to come save you and become the grounded, loving, wise inner parent you always needed.

This work changes everything, because the way you care for yourself becomes the blueprint for how you show up in every relationship. You heal the past, rewrite the present, and finally create a future that feels safe, whole, and aligned. When you give her what she needed back then, you give *you* what you need *right now*. But to really tell you about this work I want to show you what it might look like to have a conversation with your inner child. Here is a conversation I had recently with my little Libba.

Me: What do you want to tell them about when I first started reconnecting with you?

Libba: I was mad. You acted like what happened to us wasn't that bad. You used to laugh about it and that hurt my feelings because it made me feel like I didn't matter. You didn't remember how scared we were. So when you were ready, I brought you to a memory so you could really see it.

Me: Yes. And when you did that I was terrified. I finally felt that old feeling. I had been avoiding seeing and feeling that because I was scared.

Libba: But when you saw it you felt it. You knew how bad it was for us.

Me: Yes. It was the most terrifying thing I've ever felt. I was feeling that as an adult. Then you showed me what it felt like to be you, feeling that feeling.

Libba: And you couldn't laugh about it anymore. You couldn't laugh because you knew

Me: Yes. I had forgotten. I made myself forget. You made me see it. See you. Thank you for letting me see. I love you for that.

Libba: I love you for letting me show you.

Me: What do you want them to know about you?

Libba: That I'm happy now. I'm free. You protect me. No one can hurt me anymore. No one can scream and hurt my body anymore. I can say no now. I can say I don't like this. I can say I want to leave or this person is not safe. You listen to me now. You say the things I want you to say out loud. I know I'm safe now because I'm with you.

Me: That makes me so happy because you deserve that. You're a hero. If it wasn't for you I wouldn't be here.

Libba: Do I have a cape?

Me: Of course.

Libba: Yay!

Me: How did you feel before I set a boundary with our sister?

Libba: Like I was with Daddy all over again. I was mad you weren't taking care of me. I was really really angry. I was sad too. I already made it through that and you wanted to do it again.

=

Me: I didn't want to.

Libba: But you kept doing it! You kept wanting her to love us but she couldn't because she was too angry and sad.

Me: You're right.

Libba: I kept telling you I didn't feel safe, that's why our tummy would hurt.

Me: Thank you for giving me that tummy ache so I knew my feelings were real. I'm sorry it took me so long to stop wanting her to love us.

Libba: It's okay. I forgive you. I love you. I'm so happy now.

Me: Thank you for letting me heal us.

Libba: I knew you would. I knew you'd come back and make it right. I love you so much.

Me: I love YOU so much. I'll come back soon, okay?

Libba: Okay, I love you! Bye!!!

Reparenting your inner child doesn't happen all at once, it happens in layers. You grow into it, slowly, through intuition, awareness, and a whole lot of self-compassion. The truth is, your inner child has way more power than you think over your reactions, your patterns, your relationships, even the way you speak to yourself. When you begin to tend to her, to really listen, something shifts. You stop reacting from old wounds and start responding from deep wisdom. This work isn't surface-level. It's sacred. It's the kind of healing that brings you back to yourself. Reparenting is the ultimate act of self-love and it changes *everything*.

If there's one truth I've learned again and again, both in my own life and in the lives of the women I work with, it's this: The emotions you felt about the events in your past don't disappear. They don't vanish just because you've decided to move on. They don't dissolve simply because you're "busy," or "strong," or "have no time to deal with it right now." Unexpressed emotion becomes embedded and lodged in your nervous system, held in your body, and woven into your identity. And most of it belongs to the little girl inside of you. The one who didn't know how to speak of her pain, who didn't feel safe enough to express her rage or confusion or heartbreak. So she held it. And then she kept holding it. And now...you are. That grief? Still in your chest. That fear? Still in your gut. That anger? Still in your jaw. You may think you've "moved on," but the body always remembers. and the longer it stays inside, the more it controls how you show up in the world, how you love, how you trust, and how you protect yourself. This is why releasing emotion is not optional on the healing path. It is *required*. Not just in passing, but intentionally.

We must choose to create safe spaces to feel what was never felt. To give voice to the unsaid. To rage, to cry, to completely fall apart if needed. To let the little girl we once were, finish the sentence she never got to say. When we do that, something incredible happens: She doesn't just release the pain. She is released *from prison*. Because when you free her, when you allow her to feel it all without shame, you free the woman you are becoming. The warrior. The truth-teller. The boundary-holder. The legacy-builder. Letting go doesn't mean falling apart. It means finally letting the old emotions move, so they no longer rule your present. Release is not weakness, release is power. And releasing what's no longer yours to carry is how the warrior within begins to rise.

The Role of the Subconscious Mind and the Little Girl

Remember that your subconscious mind runs ninety-five percent of your life. That means that most of your beliefs, behaviors, and habits are automated, driven by early childhood programming. If you learned that love had to be earned, or if you believed that your needs were too much...If you were told to stop crying, be quiet, stay small...Those beliefs didn't just disappear. They became the code running in the background. That's why inner child work is so transformational. Because when you heal the original wound, you rewrite the code. Tools like Rapid Transformational Therapy, hypnotherapy, and inner child meditations go straight to the subconscious mind. They help you release old imprints and install new, empowering beliefs.

When your inner little girl feels seen, loved, and protected, you start to take risks again. You stop apologizing. You speak up. You create. You laugh from your belly. You say yes to things that light you up. You say no to things that drain you. And that voice inside that used to whisper, "You're too much," gets replaced with, "You're amazing." This is where the warrior lives. Not in pushing harder, but in loving deeper and in choosing yourself; in becoming the woman you were always meant to be. You become a Warrior Woman. Not someone who's pushing through, crazy busy, and never resting, but the most powerful, authentic version of you. The one that makes all decisions from her gut without questioning it; the woman who trusts herself implicitly, shines like a disco ball, and leads with a compassionate open heart.

The Power of Visualization:

Visualization is one of the most powerful tools we have for transformation because the mind and body don't know the difference between something vividly imagined and something actually experienced. Elite athletes have used this for decades, mentally rehearsing every movement, every breath, and every moment of victory. Why? Because the body responds to those mental images as if they were real. The same neurons fire. The same muscles engage. It's powerful, embodied practice. But here's the thing: Most of us are already using visualization, we're just using it *against* ourselves. We're visualizing worst-case scenarios. We're rehearsing rejection, failure, and catastrophe. We call it worry, but it's really *reverse manifestation*. It's asking for what you don't want. When you flip that script and start visualizing your healing, your success, and your joy, your entire nervous system begins to respond in kind. Healing becomes not just possible, but *inevitable*. Because the body believes what the mind repeatedly shows it. Visualization brought my little girl back to me. Let it bring your little girl back to you.

Guided Visualization and Reflection: Meeting Her Again

Here's a visualization you can use to meet your little girl: lizsvatek.com/book-visualization

Grab your journal. Breathe. Then answer:

- At what age does your little girl need to be loved the most?
- What did she need back then that she never received?
- What has she been trying to tell you through your patterns of behavior? What have you been asking of other people that you need to give yourself?
- If you could speak to her now, what would you say?
- What can you give her now to help her feel safe?

Reparenting Promises

Choose 3 from the list below or write your own:

- I promise to rest when I'm tired.
- I promise to use my voice, even when it shakes.
- I promise to protect my peace.
- I promise to stop abandoning myself to make others comfortable.
- I promise to play.
- I promise to be proud of myself, often.

=

The Warrior Woman Appears

The Warrior Woman knows that vulnerability is power. She knows that safety comes from within. And that little girls need to feel all the feelings they need to feel. That Warrior is already inside of you, but she's been waiting for the girl. She's waiting to feel safe, protected, and finally loved. Because when the girl heals, the warrior can rise. Not in fear. Not in proving her worth. But in peace. And from that place? You are limitless.

Now that you are understanding what your little girl needs to feel safe, it's time to address any fear that is still lingering and to use that fear as fuel. Fear doesn't mean "don't proceed." It means, "something big is on the other side of this." And this is where we step into our next chapter. Because once you reframe your story, and begin healing the girl so the warrior can appear, the next step is learning how to own your power. This is when you begin to work with fear and unleash your inner warrior.

Chapter 6

Unleashing Your Inner Warrior by Moving Through Fear

"Fear is like a giant fog. It sits on your brain and blocks everything–real feelings, true happiness, real joy. They can't get through that fog. But you lift it, and buddy, you're in for the ride of your life."

- BOB DIAMOND, "DEFENDING YOUR LIFE"

Fear is not your enemy. We've been taught to believe that fear is something to conquer, to eliminate, and to push aside so we can be "fearless." But what if I told you that fear isn't a problem? What if fear was actually a messenger, a guide, and a signal from your deepest self that something needs attention? Fear is not here to stop you. It's here to give you a message, and when we stop treating it as the villain, we can learn to work with it, instead of against it. Fear is often misunderstood. We think it's a sign we should turn back, that something is wrong. But in reality, fear is just a heightened awareness that something significant is happening. Fear is wise. It's bringing us wisdom and guidance if we can get ourselves still enough to listen. There are three core types of fear:

- Survival Fear: The fear that keeps us physically safe. This is hardwired into us, it's why we don't walk into traffic or touch a hot stove.

- Conditioned Fear: The fears we've inherited from society, our parents, or past experiences. The fear of failure. The fear of judgment. The fear of not being enough.
- Expansion Fear: The fear that shows up when you're about to step into a bigger version of yourself. This is the fear that whispers, "Who do you think you are?" just before you do something bold.

Not all fear is the same, and when we learn to identify it, we can learn to move through it instead of letting it stop us. We can receive the message it's bringing.

When I ask women I am coaching to rise up to unleash the inner Warrior Woman, they sometimes look at me sideways. After all, they've come to me feeling pretty beat down by life, tired from a lack of boundaries, and confused about what to do next. When you're looking to transform yourself, reinvent, and move into your legacy, it's important to remember that there was a time when you were fierce. There was a time when you didn't second-guess yourself. A time when you spoke up, stood tall, and chased after what you wanted without hesitation. For most women like yourself who want to keep growing and living their legacy, they live with a fire inside of them; a boldness that made them believe anything was possible that dimmed over time. So many of us had big dreams, loud opinions, and an unwavering confidence in who we were and what we deserved. And then? Life happened. Responsibilities, heartbreaks, expectations, and disappointments chipped away at that fire. We learned to shrink, to quiet our voices, and to accept what was handed to us instead of fighting for what we wanted. But the truth is that fire never went out, even if it dimmed to almost nothing, it's still inside. And now? It's time to reignite it.

There is immense power in remembering that bold version of yourself; the feisty, passionate woman you once were. She was unafraid to take up space, to challenge authority, to fight for what she wanted. She didn't let anyone tell her she wasn't good enough, smart enough, or worthy enough. When you reconnect with her, you tap into a part of yourself that refuses to settle, that remembers your dreams, that still believes in your ability to change your own life. The wisdom of adulthood is valuable, but when you can combine it with the untamed spirit of your younger self, you become unstoppable. You don't just reclaim who you were, you unleash the warrior within you that was never truly lost, just waiting to be called back into battle.

I was sixteen and in the middle of my junior year of high school when my mom casually mentioned we were moving into my stepfather's house in a matter of weeks. I don't know why I didn't see this coming, but this meant we were not just moving houses, we were moving states. Yes, my mom was marrying my stepfather, which, as our finances were dwindling, was a blessing. But we were also leaving behind everything I had ever known; my home, my friends, and the public school I adored. Ironically I would be attending the high school whose lacrosse team was the one we vowed to beat each season, and we lost each time. Out of *all* the schools, I couldn't fathom going there.

I felt trapped and overcome with fear. *What was going to happen to me? If I didn't have my friends, who would be looking out for me? These girls at our rival school were never going to accept me.* Now that my Mom was getting married she was ready to move on. She wanted a fresh start, while I was trying desperately to get back what I lost. I was shocked when my mom and new stepfather suggested this move like it was no big deal. They had no idea that removing the little stability I had throughout my growing up, my friends and my school, would affect me so greatly. It felt like another hit I should take and be quiet about, but I was different by the time I was sixteen. My father was no longer around to silence me. All the unexpressed rage was rising to the surface. I tried to plead my case to

=

my mom and stepfather, but there really was no other answer. We couldn't keep our house, and my stepfather wasn't selling his. After all these years of feeling like I was keeping my family afloat, and keeping our dark secrets, this truly felt like a slap in the face. *When would it feel like my life was my own? When would someone put my needs first?* I was sad that my mom and stepfather were so unwilling to see any other possible solutions, but they were resigned and somewhat cavalier about it all, acting like I was changing a shirt, not a school. But something started building, a rage about how unfair this all was. I wasn't going down without a fight.

Up until that point I had never asked for help. My parents were unavailable and didn't have the capacity to help me while I was growing up. When I would ask, there would always be a reason they couldn't help me and it made me feel worthless. I learned asking for help meant disappointment. Soon, I was the one who handled it all, and asking for help only meant weakness to me. There was a power in needing no one, but also a deep loneliness, but this time I was desperate. I was afraid to ask for help, but I needed someone to hear me and help me. I went to my guidance counselor and broke down in tears. I told her everything about how unfair it was, how much I wanted to stay at my school, and how my parents weren't listening to me or respecting my needs. I spoke passionately about a lifetime of being disregarded and wanting to be heard. I told her I knew I had rights, most importantly, the right to finally be happy. She listened intently and didn't interrupt once, even when I cursed for emphasis. And then? She did something that I'm pretty sure was illegal and would never happen today. She looked at me and said, "We'll find a way." A few days later she called me into her office again. She helped me fight by going to the principal herself, arguing my case, and asking him to make a special allowance. She arranged for me to secretly commute to my high school from another state; something that should have been impossible, but she made it happen. She got it all approved. It was done. I was staying put.

I was in tears when I received the news. I couldn't believe that she heard me, that she cared enough to go to bat for me, and that she took me seriously. That was step one. Next we had to get my parents on board. My guidance counselor called a meeting and did most of the talking. She helped me convince my parents that this was the best plan to insure my success academically and emotionally. Looking back, I still don't know exactly how she did it, but suddenly the impossible became possible. I remember she looked me in the eyes and said, "You will drive here from your new home, and we're not going to say anything about it to anyone who doesn't already know." It was our secret, and most people never knew. I got to stay at my high school. I got to graduate with my friends. I got to have my life the way I wanted it for the first time. She made me the priority, and it felt really good; all because I *finally* spoke up and asked for help.

That was my "Erin Brockovich" moment, the moment I learned that my voice mattered. That fighting for myself was not just possible, but necessary. I realized that letting fear stop me was a choice. I didn't want to let someone else dictate my life, so I took radical responsibility for it myself. I made a choice, I stood up, and I won. I'm proud of that sixteen-year-old girl who cared enough about herself to speak up. And that girl? She's still inside me, and your little girl is with you, too. She's been waiting for you to remember her. To call on her strength. To let her take the lead once again. Because she knows what you're capable of. She knows you are a warrior, and it's time for you to remember it, too.

=

Reflection & Exercise: How Fear Keeps You Stuck

Fear loves comfort zones. It thrives in familiarity. It tells you that staying where you are is safer than stepping into the unknown. But the cost of letting fear run your life is massive. It keeps you small. You don't apply for the opportunity. You don't speak up. You don't take the leap.

It reinforces self-doubt. Every time you listen to fear instead of your own inner voice, you reinforce the belief that you can't handle risk. It stops you from living fully. How many dreams have you let pass because fear told you it wasn't the right time? Fear isn't the problem, it's how we respond to it that makes the difference.

Fear is the messenger and it's asking for three things: safety, boundaries, and healing.

Fear is a response to perceived danger. Instead of ignoring it, ask yourself this question: What would make me feel safe right now? Safety can look like setting boundaries, taking small steps, or self-soothing practices like breathwork and movement. Here are three examples of how to manage fear:

1. **Reframe Your Fear:** Instead of saying, "I'm scared," try saying, "I'm expanding." Fear often appears right before a breakthrough. Recognize it as a sign you're growing, not failing.

2. **Talk to Your Fear:** Ask it, "What are you trying to protect me from?" Fear usually has a reason for showing up. Acknowledge it. Honor it. Receive the wisdom from it.

3. **Move Yourself Through Fear:** Fear hates massive leaps, but it can handle tiny steps. What's one small move you can make today to step toward what you want?

You were never meant to be fearless. You were meant to be brave. Fear will always be there, whispering doubts, and trying to keep you in the known. But you are bigger than your fear. You are the warrior who moves forward anyway. You're the woman who feels the fear and does it anyway, slowly and safely. So the next time fear shows up, don't run. Don't shrink. Turn toward it and say, "I see you. I hear you. But I choose to rise." Because that's what warriors do.

That moment in high school changed something in me. It was the first time I refused to accept someone else's decision about my life. It was the first time I realized that power wasn't something given, it was something taken. It was the first time I understood that when people don't listen to you, you don't shrink. You don't give up. You find another way. Because here's the thing: Power doesn't always come from authority. Sometimes, it comes from persistence. Some rules are meant to be challenged, rewritten, or outright broken. When someone tells you NO, you can create your own YES.

That was the moment I learned how to advocate for myself. But the real lesson? It wasn't just about me. That experience planted a fire inside me, a fire that would grow into my life's work. Because now? I don't just advocate for myself. I advocate for women. Not just for the ones I coach, but for all women and girls everywhere. I'm on the advisory board of the She Angels Foundation, championing women-led initiatives with co-founders Catherine Curry-Williams and Catherine Gray. In my coaching and community, I help women become the boldest, brightest, and most powerful versions of themselves. I stand beside them the way my guidance counselor once stood beside me, helping them fight for what they deserve, break the rules when necessary, and demand their seat at the table.

One of the biggest lessons I will carry with me from this work is that the little girl versions of ourselves are our greatest allies. I came to understand and honor the little version of me more and more as I healed. I saw her as a hero. She was the girl who took the magic mirror during a

=

taping of Romper Room and called her own name. She was the girl who started a clowning and magic business at the age of ten, and even had business cards! She was the girl who felt like she was special and was here for big things, even when she had no evidence it could be true. And that sixteen-year-old girl who refused to be silenced? She never left. She's the one who pushes me forward today, and is helping me write this book. She's the one who won't let me shrink. She's the one who reminds me that I have a voice, and I damn well better use it. And if you listen closely? Your high school teenager is still inside you, too. She's waiting for you to stop ignoring her. She's waiting for you to stop playing small. She's waiting for you to fight for her the way she always fought for you. Because you were never meant to be quiet. You were never meant to settle. You were always meant to take up space.

The truth is that fear is meant to be fuel. It's wisdom from the deepest part of us. It's asking for healing. It's asking you to shine your light into that darkness to help your soul evolve. The soul doesn't label things as good or bad, it's all a chance for you to ascend into something greater. Fear is a chance for you to rise into the woman you're here to become.

Two weeks before my wedding, my maid of honor, who was also my best friend, tried to back out. This was only one of many things that were causing me to wake up in the middle of the night. My wedding had become the ultimate boundary reset. I boldly asked for my father and stepfather to walk me down the aisle together, despite the fact that my stepfather despised my father. I was holding up a boundary with my sister now that I had Brett in my life, and keeping our contact limited to safe spaces. I was making wedding day choices my mother didn't like, asking a friend to sing for us as we walked down the aisle, getting married outside and not in a church, and having a reverend marry us that didn't have a congregation. And all through this, my closest friendship with my maid of honor was coming to an end.

I saw the cracks in the armor, but when Brett proposed, Lisa broke down. When she witnessed Brett propose on New Years Eve, I ran over and showed her my ring. Instead of congratulating me, she said, "What if I never get married?" From there things only got worse. She couldn't hold space for my happiness, it only reminded her about what she didn't have. I asked her to honor her commitment to be in my wedding, telling her it would create more drama for her to back out. She already knew my sister, mother, father, and stepfather were wild cards. She reluctantly agreed, but on my wedding day she was fake and rude. It felt wrong to be marrying the man I loved with a pure heart while this darkness was so close by. I worked hard to focus all of my attention and energy on Brett and enjoy it all, but looking back, I had let fear take over. I let my ego tell me that what things looked like was more important than how they felt. I let fear win which left my soul defeated.

There comes a point in every healing journey when it's time to **demote the ego and promote the soul**. The ego is loud, reactive, and obsessed with control. It wants to keep you safe, but its version of "safe" is often just a cage wrapped in fear. The ego will convince you to play small, stay silent, and overthink every move. It will whisper, *"What if you fail? What will they think? Who do you think you are?"* Because the ego fears expansion. But the soul? The soul is steady, soft, and certain. It doesn't need to scream, because it already knows. The soul doesn't operate from fear, it operates from truth. When you promote the soul to CEO of your life, everything shifts. You stop reacting and start responding. You stop chasing and start receiving. You don't silence the ego, you just stop letting it run the show, and that's when the real magic begins.

What if I had let my soul lead in that moment when my best friend told me she wanted to step down as a bridesmaid? What if I let the fear reveal its wisdom? Maybe I would have let her step down, and maybe I would have asked someone else to step in who was truly invested in my

=

happiness. Maybe, I would have looked at my bridesmaids with love instead of fear. If I had let her step down, I wouldn't have had to work so hard to feel the way I wanted to feel at my wedding. I would have felt more free to be vulnerable and open without her there. What if I believed that my wedding wasn't going to be ruined if she stepped down? What if I believed that I didn't need a maid of honor because I was *made of honor*. What if I had chosen to honor my heart and found that my soul was the answer? I would have known then that my worth was non-negotiable, and not based on who was standing behind me. Then, rather than forcing myself to focus on my love for Brett so that I could have an incredible wedding, I could have focused on loving and honoring myself and become limitless. Then, no matter who or what happened at my wedding, I would have been safe.

Understanding where fear is running the show and leading your life is not only crucial to your transformation, it's life changing. Seeing where you need safety, and then choosing to prioritize that, changes the game. Extracting the wisdom from fear lets the healing begin, and then you can make choices from what feels good in your soul which is *always* a win.

Exercise: The Fear Inventory - Transforming Fear into Fuel

Step 1: Call It Out

Grab your journal. Breathe. Tune in.

Write down: *What am I afraid of right now?*

This can be fear of failure, success, rejection, being seen, being too much, not being enough...

List them all. Don't filter. Let the raw truth pour out.

Step 2: Get Honest About the Cost

For each fear, ask:

- *What has this fear kept me from doing, saying, or becoming?*
- *What dreams have I delayed because of this fear?*
- *What relationships or opportunities have I missed out on?*

Step 3: Find the Fear Beneath the Fear

Go deeper. Most surface fears are masks. Ask yourself: *What is this fear really about?*

Often, fear of failure is really fear of being unloved. Fear of visibility is fear of judgment or abandonment. Write it out.

Step 4: Flip the Script

Choose one of your deepest fears and write:

What would be possible if I moved through this? Who would I become on the other side? Then write a new belief that supports your expansion. For example: I'm not afraid of failure—I'm afraid of growing too big for the life I've settled for. And I'm ready to expand.

Step 5: Warrior Ritual - Declare It

Stand up. Place your hand on your heart. Say out loud:

> *"I am done letting fear run the show. I am a warrior now. I choose courage over comfort, power over perfection, and expansion over excuses. When I move through fear. I move toward freedom."*

=

Guided Reflection Prompts

- What is the fear that has quietly followed me for years?
- How has fear disguised itself as logic or responsibility in my life?
- What part of me is trying to be protected through this fear? Is it time to release that protection?
- What would my inner warrior do today if she wasn't afraid?

The Firewalk Visualization

Imagine you're standing at the edge of a firewalk. The coals are burning. The heat rises. Your heart is pounding, not because you're weak, but because you're alive. That fire in front of you? It's every fear you've ever carried. It's every voice that has said you're not enough. Every time you abandon yourself to keep the peace is in those flames. Every limiting belief tries to convince you to turn back. Imagine yourself walking across the fire, being able to intentionally get to the other side. You reach the other side victorious and unscathed.

Here's the truth no one tells you: Fear is the initiation. You don't wait for the fear to go away. You walk through it. And on the other side? You rise. You become the version of yourself that fear was trying to protect you from; the one who's bold, fully expressed, and wide open to life. And the wildest part? Once you cross the fire once...you realize you can do it again, and again, and again. Because transformation is not a one-time event. It's a way of being. You don't just rise once. You rise, and rise again. And now, warrior woman, it's time to shed the roles that no longer fit. It's time to loosen the grip on who you were. **It's time to reinvent, reclaim, and rise.**

Chapter 7

Reinvent, Reclaim, Rise, REPEAT!

You may write me down in history
With your bitter, twisted lies,
You may trod me in the very dirt
But still, like dust, I'll rise.

- MAYA ANGELOU

For years, maybe even decades, you've been defined by your roles. The caretaker. The achiever. The fixer. The good daughter. The devoted partner. The sacrificing mother. The dependable friend. You've poured yourself into everyone and everything else, and now, for the first time in a long time, the question lingers: **What do you want?** Not what's expected of you. Not what you "should" be doing. Not what keeps the peace. But **YOU- who are YOU now?** This is the moment most women fear. Because when you strip away the roles, the expectations, the labels, what's left? If this question scares you, good. That means something inside you is ready to shift.

The version of you that is exhausted by all the doing, that is suffocating under a life that feels too heavy, the version of you that's screaming for something **more**; she's ready to rise. This is the chapter where you **wake up**. Where you **break the mold**. Where you **stop**

waiting for the right time, for permission, for clarity, and start making a move. Because reinvention doesn't happen when you think about it. It happens when you do it.

When I turned forty-nine, I hit a wall. Not just a small "I-need-a-little-change" moment, a "burn-it-all-down-and-start-over" moment. I looked around at my life, at everything I had built, and at all the roles I had perfected, and felt an ache so deep it scared me. I had spent my whole life doing what was "right." I had spent decades checking the boxes. But now? I felt like a ghost in my own life. I knew something had to change, but I had no idea what. I felt like I was being compressed in a vice. On one side I wanted more, and on the other side I kept telling myself to just be grateful.

Gratitude is powerful, but when misused, it can become a prison disguised as peace. For years, I used gratitude as an excuse to stay exactly where I was. *I should be grateful for what I have,* I'd think to myself every time something deeper stirred. Every time I felt the ache for more, and every time I felt the pull of my purpose, the whispers of doubt would surface. I weaponized gratitude to keep myself small. I wore it like armor to protect myself from disappointment, from risk, and from being seen. Gratitude gave me permission to avoid fear. It let me bypass discomfort. It became a justification for not asking for more, not leaping, and not claiming the life I secretly knew was meant for me.

Women do this all the time. We say, "I'm so lucky," while quietly dying inside. We list our blessings while ignoring the yearning. We confuse gratitude with permission to settle. But true gratitude isn't supposed to trap us, it's supposed to free us. Gratitude is an emotion, not a contract. It's a feeling, not a reason to stay stuck. You can be grateful *and* ready for more. You can be thankful *and* wildly ambitious. You can appreciate where you are *and* still crave expansion. That's not selfish. That's soul-aligned. The truth is, the version of me who used gratitude as a shield was scared. Scared of her own bigness. Scared of her power. Scared of what might happen if she actually let herself want what she wanted. But the day I realized I was using gratitude to avoid growth was the day I reclaimed my fire. Because yes, I was grateful. But I was also done shrinking.

I was working in luxury marketing, a job I was good at, paid well for, and surrounded by amazing women co-workers. But deep down, I realized it wasn't fulfilling me. I tried to stay focused on hitting goals, being a team player, and enjoying the camaraderie...until things shifted. A few men were added to the team, and suddenly the dynamic changed. Collaboration turned into competition. I started being micromanaged, my ideas were dismissed, and the energy became heavy. Every meeting felt draining. I was drowning in tasks that didn't matter and I could feel something in me pulling away. I didn't want to do this anymore, but I had no idea what came next. I knew I needed guidance from someone who could truly understand where I was, so I had lunch with my friend Sarina. Somewhere between the laughter and truth-telling, she said something that changed everything. We were talking about our future career plans when Sarina asked a question I wasn't expecting.

"Have you ever thought about starting a podcast?" I gave her a confused look while she continued talking. "Seriously, this podcast I've been listening to has been life changing, and the other day I had kind of a crazy thought. You should start a podcast! You'd be great at it!"

"What? No, that's crazy. And what exactly is a podcast, anyway? Is it something you listen to or watch? And where do I listen?" She laughed and showed me the purple "podcast" icon already installed on my phone.

"Has this been here the whole time?" I had literally never noticed this application that came preinstalled on my phone. I started entertaining the idea of starting a podcast. I didn't have any idea how to do it, I was just considering it. I was just curious. It wasn't a "hell no," but it wasn't a "hell yes," either. I started listening to podcasts and loving all the content they provided. Later that year I hosted a women's empowerment event, and

=

that was a good thing because I was still in that marketing job feeling anything but empowered. It was at that event that I met a woman who excitedly told me that she was starting a podcast. She was smiling ear to ear, beaming with excitement, and I was irritated. Annoyed. No...I was jealous! I asked her what she knew about podcasting and she admitted, "Nothing! I'm just going to do it!" *Well,* I thought, *she's clearly crazy. I mean who just launches a podcast without knowing exactly how to do it?* The fact that she thought she could do that bothered me even more. *Why couldn't I be that confident and unbothered?*

After the event, a kind woman named Becky offered me a ride to a nearby restaurant where a few of us were meeting for dinner. On the way, I made small talk.

"So, what do you do?"

"I'm in marketing and I help people launch podcasts," she said with a big smile on her face. I practically choked.

"You're kidding me," I said, feeling the Universe hit me over the head with a velvet hammer. "That's so weird, I've been thinking about starting a podcast, but I have zero idea where to begin. I think I want to do it... but I'm not ready." Then, without really thinking, I added, "If you reach out to me in January, I'll do it." We laughed, went on with our evening, and didn't talk about it again. We exchanged numbers and emails, but honestly I assumed I'd never hear from her again. But on January 2nd, Becky reached out. There was no small talk this time, just the link to pay and one line that read, "Let's launch your podcast!" I stared at that message like it was a dare. My stomach was flipping. I didn't know if I'd be good at podcasting. I didn't have a master plan. I didn't even know what I'd talk about. But I did know one thing: I needed something new, and something that lit me up. And this, whatever "this" was, had that spark. So I took a deep breath, leaned into the fear and excitement buzzing in my chest, and clicked "pay." Was I terrified? Absolutely. My thoughts were loud. *What if I fail? What if people think I'm ridiculous? What if I have no idea what I'm doing?* But here's the thing: There's a big difference between **fear** and **danger**. This wasn't dangerous. It was just...big. New. Uncharted. And in that moment, I realized: The fear of failing was real, but the fear of staying the same? That was even bigger.

I had to get honest with myself. There was a part of me that wasn't just craving change, it was craving *impact*. I wanted to make a statement, not for attention, but because something inside me knew I was here to leave a mark that went beyond my own life. I wanted to show up bigger, louder, and more powerfully. I wanted to stop shrinking and start building something that would last. Something that mattered. The older I got, the louder that inner voice became. I had wisdom to share, and it was real, hard-won wisdom. I was finally ready to stop keeping it quiet. I wanted to have the conversations I wasn't hearing. I wanted to speak the truth and hear it echoed back by other women walking through fire and transformation. Starting the podcast was a leap of faith. And even though I've been leaping my whole life, this leap felt different. The older I got, the scarier it became. The fear of judgment, of being "too much," of falling flat on my face...it was *loud*. The fear of failing publicly was almost paralyzing. But the fear of *not* doing it? The fear of staying small, hidden, and unheard? That was worse. And so I jumped while I was shaking and scared, but knowing somewhere deep down that this leap was the beginning of legacy.

It's normal to question everything when you're out of your comfort zone because fear is trying to stop you from doing something new. But fear is not a stop sign, it's a green light. It's a sign you're on the right track, because if you're uncomfortable and scared, you're evolving. Looking back now I can see how God, the Universe, Spirit, or whatever you may call it, was conspiring in my favor. Having that woman announce she was starting a podcast, and feeling that jealousy, let me know how badly I wanted to take that leap. Meeting Becky was the perfect way to get started

=

because she could guide me through the process. Without her coaching me and cheering me on I never would have done it. Remember this: There's always a woman who has walked the path before us, we just have to take her hand. And so I did. The Universe was calling me into my legacy, and I answered the call.

And still, with all this guidance, there was failure. Even though I hired a podcast expert, the process was messy and imperfect. I fumbled through tech issues, I forgot to hit "record" multiple times and had to call guests back to re-record. There were times when I wanted to give up. The doubt about my ability, the technology I had to learn and relearn, the way I cringed when I first heard the sound of my own voice. But I kept going. Conversations with Warrior Women launched, amid the pandemic no less, and I was proud. The interviews were a lifeline to me and so many other women who needed to hear stories of resilience and empowerment. I was leaping, and loving this new adventure, even when it wasn't perfect. And then one day I looked up, and my little experiment, the thing I almost talked myself out of, was ranked in the top one-and-a-half percent of podcasts globally. When I saw that ranking my jaw dropped, and the tears came. How easy it would have been to ignore this nudge, this curiosity, and the feeling of wanting something new. How easy it would have been to quit and not follow through. How easy it would have been to say no. This one decision, this one yes to what was scaring me, led to where I am today. But I had to keep showing up, taking that messy action, to get there. One small, messy decision had set off a chain reaction of reinvention. Because the truth is, you don't need to have a perfect plan, or have everything figured out, or be good at something before you begin. You just need to leap.

Here's what no one tells you about reinvention: It can feel awkward, uncomfortable, and completely wrong at first. At first, you're pretty sure that you are the crazy one. The whole reinvention process made me question everything. I had decided to follow the yellow brick road and I wanted to turn back! I would ask myself, *Who do you think you are? What if you fail? What if people judge you?* My advice to you is this: You will hear those thoughts. Keep going anyway. Because the only way to get to the other side, to the version of you that feels fully alive, is to go through the discomfort of becoming her; the woman that has something she's proud of.

Reinvention is contagious. When we embark on something new it inspires others. And it sets off a chain reaction. That leap when I started the podcast led to another leap. And this one was even bigger. A Quantum Leap! On one of my podcast episodes I featured a spiritual teacher named Tracy Litt. She floored me when she asked, "What if your thoughts are just options?" I am rarely speechless, but that question stopped me cold. *What did she mean my thoughts were options? I wasn't choosing to have my mind racing. Was I? Could I actually make it stop? Have a peaceful mind? Choose what I wanted to think?* I was once again curious, excited, and I felt fear enter the ring.

One thing I've started to recognize is when I have that feeling, when fear is showing up, I'm on the edge of my next big leap. Rather than panicking I start to get curious. I had learned to leap again and I didn't want to stop. After our recording, I began to read Tracy's book *Worthy Human: Because You Are the Problem and the Solution*. I started to watch her videos, and immerse myself in her methods and practices. Later that year I attended her retreat where I learned more about her work. I had always loved personal growth since I was a teenager. I loved reading, watching, or listening to any stories or teachings that could improve my life. I looked to spiritual teachers, coaches and thought leaders like Tony Robbins, Oprah, Marianne Williamson, Iyanla Vanzant. I devoured all their wisdom. I realized that a passion for evolution and growth was a constant in my life.

At the retreat that Tracy was hosting I was able to immerse myself in personal growth on a deeper level than ever before. I was in community

=

and sisterhood. I loved all the women I was meeting who were like-minded seekers and their stories of transformation were incredible and inspiring. I had been told before that I should be a life coach, but refused to do it. *There are too many coaches,* I would tell myself, *everyone's a life coach. What do I have that's special?*

But when she offered a coaching certification in her work, something felt right. I finally felt like I had clarity around what I wanted to do. I did want to be a coach, and now I felt like I had the material I wanted to teach. I signed up on the spot. This was one of the first times I really invested in myself. It was a "hell yes" decision and I didn't question it. When I signed up for the coaching certification, I put ten-thousand dollars on a credit card as if it was normal practice for me. Rather than mentioning this to my husband, I didn't tell him right away. Not because I was hiding it, but because I wanted to keep it just for me. I wanted to enjoy the fact that I made a decision with no one else in mind but myself. And...I didn't want to break the spell of the decision. I knew if I asked permission, ran it by him, over-explained, or asked for validation, I would talk myself out of it. So instead, I just dove in head first.

Later that year at the coaching immersion event, I started becoming close friends with the women in my coaching cohort. I felt excited and nervous about practicing the tools and techniques we were learning. After getting up in front of everyone, I admitted to the other women that I hadn't coached a single person yet. When I was practicing that coaching moment, it was my first time *actually* coaching. They were shocked. They assumed I was already thriving in my coaching business. Something about that gave me courage. They had all been coaching for years and they thought I was one of them. *Maybe I really was made for this,* I thought.

That night we all went down to the beach at our hotel. We put our feet in the sand to watch the sunset, proud of ourselves and how much we'd grown over the weekend. I had expressed to my friend Stacie that I was afraid to coach because I "wasn't a coach," so she had me write, "I'm not a coach" in the sand. And then? We let the waves wash it away. That was the moment I let go of the old version of myself. The moment I claimed something bigger. And here's what I want you to know: You don't become the new version of you by waiting to feel ready. You'll never "feel" ready. You become HER by deciding. Ready isn't a feeling. It's a *decision*. I decided, and a new adventure began.

Rewrite the Rules. Redefine Success.

Women are taught that success looks like:

- A perfect marriage.
- A stable career.
- A beautifully decorated home.
- Being **nice, agreeable, and easy to be around.**

But what if that version of success is keeping you stuck?

What if **success for you** looks like...

- Reinventing yourself.
- Starting something new with **zero experience**.
- Traveling alone.
- Writing a book.
- Launching your business.
- Moving somewhere that feels more like **you**.
- Saying **no** without guilt.
- Taking up space.

I want you to define success on your terms. I want you to stop living by rules that weren't made for you. I want you to build a life that lights you up, not one that just looks good on the outside.

=

REINVENT, RECLAIM, RISE, REPEAT!

Your Next Steps (Yes, This Is Homework)

Reinvention doesn't happen **in your head**. It happens **through action**.

1. Guided Reflection Prompts:

- **If no one was judging**, what would you do?
- If you had **zero obligations**, no one to please, nothing to prove...
- If you knew **you wouldn't fail**...
- If you could **reinvent yourself completely...What would you do?**

Write it down. **No filtering.** No worrying about what's "realistic."

2. Take One Bold Action This Week

- **Book the class.**
- **Make the call.**
- **Start the damn thing.**

1. Where in your life are you using gratitude to silence what you really want to do?

Are there places you're convincing yourself to stay small because "you should be thankful"? Be honest. Wanting more isn't ungrateful, it's legacy calling!

2. What would change if gratitude became your fuel, not your ceiling?

Imagine letting your gratitude be the launching pad instead of the finish line. What would you do differently?

3. What are you truly yearning for right now?

Forget what you *should* want. Forget what you think you're allowed to ask for. What is your soul whispering?

Affirmation:

I am grateful for where I am. And I trust the part of me that wants more. Gratitude is not the end. It is the beginning.

The Moment You Stop Playing Small

You will always find a reason not to do the thing you want to do. You will always feel "not ready." You will always wonder if you're too old, too late, too much, or not enough. Do it anyway. Because the moment you take that leap, and the moment you choose yourself, everything changes. And you have to keep choosing yourself over and over again. Reinvention is not a one-time event. It is a way of life.

You will reinvent, reclaim, and rise, again and again and again. And each time, you will get closer to the most fully alive, fully expressed, version of you. You know that quiet voice inside? The one that nudges you, pulls you, and whispers when something feels off or lights you up? The one you've probably spent years second-guessing, overanalyzing, or flat-out ignoring? That voice is your superpower. But somewhere along the way, we were taught to doubt ourselves. To seek permission before making a move. To trust the "experts" instead of our own knowledge. We've been conditioned to believe that intuition is irrational, that if we can't explain it, measure it, or prove it, it must not be real.

But here's what I've learned: Logic is useful, but intuition is powerful.

Every big leap I've ever taken, whether it be the podcast, my coaching business, or the bold decisions that shaped my life as a Warrior Woman, didn't come from a spreadsheet. They came from a feeling. A knowing. A whisper that said, "This is it. Go." And every time I ignored that whisper? I ended up exactly where I didn't want to be.

So in this next chapter, we're tuning in. We're ditching overthinking for inner knowing. We're shifting from seeking external validation to

=

trusting ourselves deeply. We're learning how to hear the whisper and, more importantly, how to follow it. Your intuition has been speaking to you all along, you just didn't know it!

Chapter 8

Trust the Whisper: Your Intuition is Your Superpower

"Something has changed within me. Something is not the same. I'm through with playing by the rules of someone else's game. Too late for second-guessing. Too late to go back to sleep. It's time to trust my instincts, close my eyes and leap!"

- ELPHABA IN "WICKED"

How many times have you known something was true, but you had no way to really prove it? Maybe it was a gut feeling that told you to take a different route, or inner nudge that warned you about someone's energy. It was a whisper in your soul that kept saying, "There's more for you than this." That wasn't a coincidence. That was your intuition. And it's time to rebuild trust with the most powerful guide you'll ever have, yourself.

For too long, we've been taught to dismiss our intuition. We've been conditioned to believe that facts, logic, and other people's opinions hold more weight than our own inner knowing. We seek validation from experts, family, partners, and friends. We poll the audience, create pros-and-cons lists, and overthink our way into exhaustion. But here's the truth: Your intuition is your most powerful decision-making tool. When you learn to trust it, you move through life with clarity, confidence, and ease. You stop outsourcing your power. You stop living by committee.

You start showing up for yourself knowing, deep in your bones, that the only validation you need is your own. I've ignored my intuition many times, and every single time, it came back to bite me. Like when I stayed in a business partnership that I *knew* deep down wasn't aligned. I felt it in my gut from the very beginning; the uneasiness, the way I second-guessed myself whenever we spoke, the moments where I felt like I had to shrink myself to keep the peace. But I ignored it because the opportunity looked good on paper.

And guess what? It turned out to be a nightmare. I lost money, energy, and time. And when it finally ended, I looked back and thought, *I knew. I knew this wasn't right. Why didn't I trust myself?* Or the time I hired a coach who had the "perfect" business model. He promised a roadmap, results, all the things. But from the very first call, something felt *off.* He was forceful, dismissive of my instincts, and kept telling me to do things that didn't feel right. But I told myself, *Maybe he knows better. Maybe I should just listen and follow the steps.* Wrong.

The whole time, I was trying to fit myself into his blueprint when my own compass was screaming, *This isn't for you.* And it wasn't. It drained me, misaligned my brand, and made me feel like I had to *be someone else* to succeed. But when I finally walked away and *did things my way,* my business exploded. I learned my lesson. My intuition isn't just a quiet whisper, it's a lighthouse trying to guide me home.

Your intuition isn't some mystical force reserved for psychics and sages, it's your built-in compass. Your gut feelings, inner nudges, and deep knowing are all ways your body and mind communicate what's right (or wrong) for you. Some people feel it as a *pull* toward something. Others experience it as a *physical sensation*, a tightness in the chest, a gut drop, or even goosebumps. For some, it's a whisper of words or images flashing in their mind. And yet, we doubt it. We tell ourselves we're imagining things, that we need more proof, that we should wait for *certainty* before we act, or that we are making it all up ourselves. But certainty doesn't come from logic alone, it comes from trusting yourself enough to move, even when you don't have all the answers. If you've ever wondered if you're feeling fear or hearing your intuition, you're not alone. The key difference? Intuition is calm. Anxiety is chaotic.

- Intuition feels like a quiet, steady knowing. Anxiety feels like a spiraling storm.
- Intuition nudges you toward truth. Anxiety shouts worst-case scenarios.
- Intuition is neutral and peaceful, even when it's guiding you to something uncomfortable. Anxiety, on the other hand, is frantic, pressured, and urgent.

The next time you're uncertain, check in with yourself. Take a deep breath and ask: Is this coming from fear, or is this my inner wisdom gently guiding me? Tip for Beginners: If it feels low, shitty, and awful that's not intuition. If it feels like shit, it's a lie.

When 2001 began, I was in a really low place. My sister was dating one of my last highschool boyfriends, someone I still cared about, and I felt like my family had abandoned me. They didn't understand how hurtful this was. They didn't get that this was the culmination of feeling invisible for my entire life. All my relationships with men were about desperately trying to be seen and loved, and now they had all ended. I was single, but what I really felt was alone. My acting and writing career was stalled out, my friendships felt fake, and I felt like I didn't want to be here anymore. I didn't want to live the way I was anymore.

And so I drove to Santa Monica, with the intention of killing myself. I had absolute certainty about this. It felt calm because I had decided. I was finally going to get some relief, and finally my family would see how much pain I had been in. I called my friend Nick, not to stop me, but to

=

let him know so someone would find me. He tried to keep me on the phone, crying and telling me not to do it. But I reminded him of how long I'd been in pain, how my family would never change, and how I couldn't do this anymore.

I arrived in Santa Monica and sat on a cliffside overlooking the ocean. I felt like shit. Lower than low. But I truly believed this was the answer. It was a sunny, beautiful day, so I tried talking to God. I started telling him how sick and tired I was of all of this. I was begging for it all to end. I had tears in my eyes, and my soul was crying out to be saved. Then, seemingly out of nowhere, a blonde surfer, probably around my same age, approached me.

"Hi, how ya doin'?" *Was he kidding?* I almost laughed. I wiped the tears away and casually smiled at him.

"Good, you?" I hoped he would notice that I was lying to his face. I wasn't even close to "good."

"Oh, I'm great! It's a beautiful day, and I'm about to go surfing with friends. It doesn't get much better than that." *Oh my God,* I thought, *Can he just get out of here so I can get back to business?* But he wasn't leaving me alone. What he said next caught me completely off guard.

"Since it's such a great day, why don't you come with me? Then we can go to lunch after?" I hesitated, but being in such a low spot mentally, it felt nice to make a brief connection with someone. "Maybe...you want to give me your number?" I couldn't believe the words that had just come out of my mouth, because only minutes earlier, I wasn't even sure I wanted to be on this Earth. Then out of nowhere this surfer walks up to me, totally oblivious to the storm I was in, and asks me out. He just saw a woman he wanted to hang out with. I actually laughed.

Here I was, spiraling in the darkest place I'd ever been... and he just wanted to know if I was free this weekend. It was bizarrely funny and honestly, it shifted something in me. His lightness snapped me out of the heaviness, just for a moment, and that moment was enough to get me through the next one. I went home, still holding the piece of paper with his number on it. It was as if God sent this boy to stop me. I told myself I'd see how I felt the next day, and, to my surprise, I felt better. Something about the innocence of that surfer wanting to spend time with me told me I was worth something. The truth is that I did want to kill myself that day, but not the way I thought. I didn't want my life to end, I wanted the identity I had embraced up to that point to end. I wanted to be someone else.

Many of us know we can't keep living the way we're living. We know that we can't keep going the way that we are, and we hate the part of ourselves that is participating in our pain. This can feel like a death of sorts. It's the death of the old identity. This happens when you no longer want to be the person who feels unloved, unworthy, and depressed. We think by killing ourselves the pain will end. But that's not what we really want. What we want is to become new. For this old identity to be killed off, so that we can be different and feel worthy again.

Many people who survive a suicide attempt describe an immediate shift in perspective. Some report feeling an intense sense of relief, and a renewed appreciation for life upon realizing they had survived. One survivor shared, "I felt as if I'd been given a new lease on life." A new lease on life? A new identity really. They became new at that moment, almost instantly. The profound impact of survival changed their outlook, and changed who they were. Like me, they started to believe that since they survived that they must matter. Statistically, nine out of ten people who attempt suicide and survive do not go on to die by suicide at a later date. Because they don't need to anymore. They're not the same person, even if they are in the same body.

If you ever find yourself at the edge, questioning whether you can keep going, or if someone you love is standing in that place of unbearable pain, I want you to remember this: You don't actually want to die. You want the pain to end. You want to kill off the version of you that's

=

exhausted, disconnected, and buried under the weight of trauma, obligation, or unhealed wounds. You want to burn down the life that no longer fits; the life built on "shoulds," survival, silence, and self-abandonment. And that is not a death wish, that is a rebirth wish. That's your soul screaming for transformation and reinvention. You are looking for a chance to live as the real you, not the version molded by pain or expectation. So please hear this: You don't need to end your life. **You need to end the chapter that's breaking your spirit.**

You get to burn the old stories. You get to lay down the armor. You get to walk away from who you were told to be, so you can rise as who you really are. The version of you that's waiting on the other side of this pain is powerful, radiant, and free. Hold on for that little girl who has suffered and has a chance to be free. Hold on for her. I thought the whisper I was hearing was to end my life, but I was wrong. Instead it was to be reborn. This was the beginning of me learning to trust myself, and hear what my soul was calling me to do.

After reconnecting with my little girl and beginning to heal the trauma from my past, by late 2021 my life was almost unrecognizable to me. I had changed almost everything in my life. By following my intuition, I had started a successful podcast, I had gotten my coaching certification, and I no longer had my sister in my life. Setting that boundary gave me the space, the confidence, and the clarity I needed. I like to think about things in terms of energetic parking spaces. When something is parked in one of your energetic spaces, nothing new can come in. It's occupying your life; mind, body, and soul. My relationship with my sister was taking up a whole energetic parking garage, and without her in my life I finally felt free to do everything my soul was calling for. I had the space and the capacity to do things that were bolder and bigger. I felt excited and more confident than ever before.

My intuition muscle was getting stronger and stronger. I was getting winks, nudges, and not just whispers, but strong gut feelings. I was beginning to follow my curiosity without judging where it would lead me. And somehow, I started to hear the word "mastermind" more and more. For years, I kept hearing about mastermind groups as the secret weapons of success for men. They were behind-the-scenes power circles where big ideas were born and major moves were made. I was intrigued, but also slightly skeptical. Were these just glorified networking events? Were they exclusive boys' clubs where the "real" business happened? The more I learned, the more fascinated I became. And then it hit me: Women had been left out of this for far too long. This is what women needed.

I went into deep research mode, devouring any information I could. I found out that the term "mastermind" was first coined by Napoleon Hill in his 1937 book *Think and Grow Rich*. As he put it, a mastermind is when "two or more minds working in harmony toward a definite objective creates a third, more powerful mind." His research on successful people of his time, including Henry Ford, Andrew Carnegie, and Thomas Edison, revealed that nearly all of them had a close-knit circle of advisors, peers, and mentors who challenged and supported them. These weren't casual friendships, they were intentional, structured groups designed to push each member toward exponential growth.

As I dug a little further, I found out that the concept of mastermind groups dated back centuries, long before Napoleon Hill. Some of the earliest known mastermind groups were intellectual and philosophical circles where great minds gathered to exchange ideas, challenge perspectives, and push innovation forward. In Ancient Greece, Socrates, Plato, and Aristotle formed what could be considered one of the first mastermind groups, engaging in deep discussions that shaped Western philosophy. During the Renaissance, artists and thinkers like Leonardo da Vinci, Michelangelo, and Galileo were part of networks that fueled creativity and scientific progress. In the eighteenth century, Benjamin Franklin created the Junto, a mastermind-style group of tradesmen and intellectuals who

=

met weekly in Philadelphia to discuss business, politics, and self-improvement. And of course, the Founding Fathers of the United States, Washington, Jefferson, Adams, and others, regularly gathered to debate and refine the ideas that would shape an entire nation. Mastermind groups have always been the breeding ground for innovation, transformation, and legacy-building. The only difference? For most of history, they were almost exclusively made up of men.

What struck me was that men had been doing this for centuries. They had been building, executing, and amassing wealth and power in these small, safe, micro communities. Masterminds weren't just launch pads, they were woven into the DNA of success. Every big company I respected, every titan of business, and even our very constitution, all began with masterminds. *But where were the women?*

Of course, women have always found ways to support each other, whether in quilting circles, book clubs, or informal kitchen-table conversations, but historically, we weren't invited into the rooms where power and strategy were happening. We weren't taught to form these alliances with the intention of collective elevation. Instead, society conditioned us to compete with each other, and to believe in the scarcity myth that there was only room for one woman at the top. Women have been sold on competition instead of collaboration, and that is complete and utter bullshit.

That's when I knew I had to create something different. I wanted a space where women didn't just gather to vent, or trade surface-level advice, but where they could rise together. A place where vulnerability met ambition, where honesty and high-level strategy could coexist, and where women could finally experience the kind of collective power that had been working for men for centuries. I wasn't just interested in starting a mastermind, I was on a mission to rewrite the narrative. Because why should women keep fighting for a seat at the table when we could just build the damn table?

And just like that, the first Warrior Women Mastermind group was formed. Well, at least it was in my mind. I had a vision and a decision to move forward with it. In order to make it happen, I had to speak as if it already was. I started talking about this mastermind group I had and what we were going to do everywhere I went. Within a few days I had women paying me and signing up. I started with a group of six women, then another group of six, then another. The Warrior Women Mastermind groups grew and grew, and before I knew it I had made six figures my first year in business. Many people doubted me, rejected my idea, and said it wasn't as valuable as I knew it was, but they were wrong. Now that original mastermind has evolved into the Wise Women Collective, a VIP, one-year experience with a retreat. As I was writing this book, I realized I had to take it even further, reach more women, and create more legacies.

I am now offering a certification for the Warrior Women Mastermind group (lizsvatek.com/certification) so that women across the country can start giving each other the kind of support that creates a legacy. This is how we change the world, one woman at a time.

My intuition used to show up as a whisper that, overtime, has turned into an assertive voice that I never ignore when I hear it. For a long time it was the whisper of wanting more meaning and purpose. It was the whisper of wanting to be seen and known for something impactful. It was the whisper of leadership, entrepreneurship, and of wanting to live in my truth. It was the whisper of wanting more depth in my friendships, in my work, and in my family. It was the whisper of my soul. Because I listened, I am now able to stay in touch with that intuition all the time, and it no longer whispers. It affirms with confidence.

=

Exercise: The Whisper That Won't Go Away

Somewhere inside of you, there's a whisper. A longing. A knowing that something more is meant for you. But have you been listening?

Close your eyes, take a deep breath, and finish these sentences:

- If I wasn't afraid of what people would think, I would...
- If I knew I wouldn't fail, I would...
- If I let myself be completely honest, I really want...

Look at your answers. Now ask yourself:

- Have I ignored or pushed these thoughts away before?
- Where do these whispers show up the most, when I'm alone, driving, lying in bed?
- What would happen if I stopped ignoring them?

Reflection:

This whisper inside of you? It's not random. It's your future self calling you forward. Write a letter from your future self, five years from now, who has listened to these whispers and made changes. What does she say to you? What has changed?

I had no proof. No roadmap. Just a whisper that kept saying, "*Do it.*" So I did. I launched my first mastermind purely on intuition. I had no idea if women would join. I had no idea if it would work. But I trusted the whisper, and then, over time, I realized women had actually held the *first* masterminds, they were called tribes.

For centuries, before business meetings and boardrooms, before networking events and industry conferences, women gathered in circles. They raised children together, cared for their communities, passed down wisdom, and navigated life's biggest challenges *as a collective.*

While history often credits men with the invention of masterminds, men like Napoleon Hill, the Founding Fathers, and the business titans who built empires, women had already been doing it for generations. Long before official titles and structured meetings, they built support systems that were vital to their survival. In tribes, women worked together to ensure the success of the whole. They pooled resources, shared knowledge, and provided guidance. They weren't competing, they were collaborating. They weren't isolated, they were interconnected. They weren't just supporting each other, they were *expanding* each other.

Somewhere along the way, society tried to rewrite the narrative. Women were conditioned to believe that success was a *solo* pursuit, that competition mattered more than collaboration, and that they had to figure it all out alone. But the truth? We were never meant to do this alone. Women *thrive* when we are in community. We always have. And the modern mastermind? It's just a return to what we've always known: We rise higher, faster, and with more joy when we rise together, as Warrior Women.

You Were Born Intuitive – Here's How to Reclaim It

Your intuition has always been there, conditioning just taught you to doubt it.

- Logic is Valuable, but Intuition is Sacred – The best decisions come from a balance of head and heart.
- Doubt & Overthinking Block Intuition – The more you second-guess, the harder it is to hear your inner wisdom.
- The More You Trust It, the Stronger It Becomes – The more you listen, the louder it gets.

That voice inside you? The one that's been whispering to you all along? It's not just real, it's your greatest superpower. And now that you're

=

listening, you'll never ignore it again. Because once you start trusting your intuition, you stop just surviving, and you start creating with purpose. You start aligning your life, your work, and your impact with something much bigger.

Guided Reflection – Strengthening Your Intuition

Take a moment, grab a journal, and ask yourself:

1. What's one time your intuition was right, but you ignored it?
2. What would have changed if you had trusted it?
3. How can you start listening more today?

Your next step? Trust the whisper. Move toward what feels right. Your intuition has been waiting for you to listen. This chapter is a turning point. Because once you fully trust yourself, your inner voice, your truth, your knowing...everything shifts. And once you unlock that power? There's no stopping you. Your legacy unfolds.

Chapter 9

Designing Your Legacy: Stop Waiting, Start Leading

"You can't choose how you're going to die, or when. You can only decide how you're going to live now."

- JOAN BAEZ

If someone asked you right now what your legacy is, would you have an answer? Most people wouldn't. Because we've been conditioned to think of legacy as something that happens later, or something we leave behind in a will, a foundation, or a name engraved on a plaque. We picture legacy as the grand gestures, the billion dollar endowments, the historic firsts, or the monuments built in someone's honor. But here's what no one tells you: Your legacy isn't just what you leave behind, it's how you live every single day.

Your legacy is the energy you're emitting, the frequency of you; it's how your soul is traveling through life. It's the way you hug your loved one a little longer when they've had a tough day. It's the way you pause before reacting in frustration, choosing compassion instead. It's the way you put yourself first knowing when you heal yourself, invest in yourself, and explore your legacy, you become the ripple effect. Want to love your partner? Your kids? Your friends? Love yourself first. You are the most important relationship you'll ever have, and that relationship affects all others.

Legacy is built in big and small moments. It's in your relationships. Do the people you care about feel safe to be themselves around you? Do your friends know you're a woman of integrity? Does your partner feel seen, not just managed? Do you give yourself compassion, trust the whispers of your intuition, and live in your fullest unique expression?

It's in the energy you bring into a room. Do people feel uplifted in your presence, or do you bring the weight of unspoken resentment? It's in your courage to change. Are you modeling reinvention, showing that it's never too late to grow? Or are you stuck in a life you outgrew, waiting for permission to want more? It's in the choices you make when no one is watching. Do you set boundaries, honor your own needs, and live in alignment with your values? Most people don't think about their legacy until it's too late. But the truth is, legacy is not someday. It's now. And the question is: Are you creating yours on purpose? Or are you living by default, letting circumstances, fear, and other people's expectations shape the story of your life? The beauty of it all? You get to decide. Right now. Today. This moment is part of your legacy. So what will you do with it?

For years, I thought I was "doing it all," and doing it well. I was running a business, raising kids, showing up for my partner and friends, and being the woman who could handle anything. And like most women, I put myself at the bottom of the list. My body could wait. My needs could wait. My health could wait. Until it couldn't. One day at a routine gynecologist appointment they checked my blood pressure and it was high. I hadn't had high blood pressure before, except when Landon was born, so we attributed it to me being late for my appointment and running too fast. But at the end of the appointment they checked it again and it was exactly the same.

This led to me being officially diagnosed with high blood pressure, getting put on blood pressure medication, and having to wear a harness heart monitor to track irregular heartbeats. The harness didn't show much, but my blood pressure was high and I needed daily medication. They also detected a small tear in the lining of my heart, something they needed to watch. This news did slow me down for a bit, but old habits of stress and pressure came back and I was once again "doing it all." To be honest, I didn't know there was another way. *Who has time to relax and do yoga when there's so much to take care of?*

I was back to my old self, constantly in survival mode, when I got a wake-up call that shook me to my core. I was at a preschool moms' holiday party, standing in the kitchen, drinking champagne, and laughing about how exhausted we all were. I turned to my friend Sarah, a powerhouse attorney, mother, and one of the most capable women I knew, and we joked about our schedules, the stress, the fact that we were both on blood pressure meds at forty.

She was telling me how she was even going back to work after this party. She was "doing it all." She was making time for her kids, working, and socializing. She was able to balance it all, or so she said. Not that it was easy, of course. She admitted she was tired, living on caffeine, wine, and adrenaline. At her high-powered job she needed to be on point, and as a mother she was the same. Something had to give, and it was often her doing the giving. We joked how we were so busy we sometimes forgot to take our heart medication. We laughed about that. The day after that conversation, she died of a stroke and two little girls were left shattered. She was forty-two years old. At her funeral I sat with all the other preschool moms, feeling incredulous; I simply couldn't believe it. *How could this happen?* I watched as her husband, her family, and her kids all admitted she was the rock, the glue, and the guiding light of the family, and now she was gone.

That was the moment it hit me. I had been treating my own life like it was going to last forever, like there would always be more time. I had been pouring into everyone else while my own well was running dry. I thought about my kids. *What kind of legacy was I leaving them if I didn't* *take care of myself? If all they saw was a woman who gave everything and left nothing for herself, what would they learn from that?* I remember watching my mom rushing around, always tending to us, and having nothing for herself. I watched her dreams denied and belittled by my father, and then, later in her life, she denied her dreams and desires herself.

So I made a decision that day, because all change starts with a decision. I decided to prioritize myself. My health, my life, my well-being. Over the years I've gotten better and better at this. Sometimes I fall back into old patterns when my children are struggling or I'm working too much, but I made a commitment to myself and I *meant* it. I decided that my health was more important, and my emotional well-being and happiness were a priority. If I fall off the wagon of putting my health first, I recommit and get right back on.

After learning and developing a few practices, I teach my clients the Morning Magic routine. One that included tapping, meditation and journaling. This is what I teach to all the women who coach with me. This is what works and keeps me feeling peaceful; mind, body and soul. But I want you to know that I went kicking and screaming into meditation. Looking back I realize how living so many years with PTSD had put me in permanent survival mode. "Doing it all" wasn't just a choice, it was a trauma response. I was doing it all to feel safe. I thought I had to control everything for my family to be safe. I didn't want to be present, or to stop and slow down, because then all the thoughts and emotions I was running away from would catch up to me.

I found the work of Dr. Joe Dispenza to be the most enlightening in terms of meditation. He has cracked the code on what ancient wisdom has been telling us for centuries: Meditation isn't just about "relaxing" or clearing your mind, it's about literally rewiring your brain, shifting your emotional state, and healing your body at a cellular level. Through his research, Dispenza has shown that deep meditation changes brainwave activity, activates the nervous system in ways that promote healing, and even rewrites the subconscious beliefs that keep us stuck. And the wildest part? He has brain scans to prove it. I've been to a few of his retreats and they are life changing.

One of the biggest takeaways from his work is that when we shift out of survival mode (stress, fear, self-doubt), and into elevated emotions like gratitude and love, our body starts producing the chemicals and hormones that heal us physically, mentally, and emotionally. Meditation isn't just "woo-woo, new age stuff," it is science-backed transformation. His research shows that people who practice meditation consistently have stronger immune systems, lower inflammation, and even experience spontaneous healings.

But Dispenza takes it even further. He teaches that when we move beyond our limiting beliefs and step into pure consciousness, we actually start influencing our external reality. His studies document people healing chronic illnesses, overcoming trauma, and manifesting massive changes in their lives, all by learning how to harness the power of their own mind. He's proving what many of us have felt intuitively: We are not victims of our past, our biology, or our circumstances. We are the creators of our reality. Meditation is not just about "zen vibes" and deep breathing, it's a tool for transformation, a direct pathway to shifting your life at the deepest level. And I can prove it.

I was able to heal that small tear in my heart lining, not with surgery, but through breathwork and meditation. When they scanned my heart again, after adopting the Morning Magic routine, the tear was no longer there. My doctor was stunned, and I knew, with absolute certainty, that this shift wasn't just about me. It was about my children watching me take care of myself and heal myself. It was about the women who watched me rise. It was about showing, not just saying, that legacy starts with how you live.

=

Meditation isn't an indulgence. It's non-negotiable. Your body only moves into rest and repair when you close your eyes and relax. And when you learn to meditate it can first feel like you're trying to tame a wild horse. Your mind will race, and it will feel uncomfortable, maybe even emotional. But if you stick with it, stay in the ring long enough, your mind will know who's boss. You'll tame the horse. You'll start to feel like meditation is a vacation from the day-to-day.

I had put off prioritizing my health and well being with the "One Day Myth." I kept telling myself that one day I'll have more time, more energy, or more freedom...but then I was still saying that years later. The truth? The perfect time wasn't coming. I had to create it. That moment at Sarah's funeral was when I made the decision to prioritize my health, which made me ask a bigger question...What else had I been putting off?

We often think of legacy as a grand achievement like a book, a business, or a foundation. But legacy isn't just about what you do, it's about how you make people feel. Right now, in this moment, your energy is leaving an imprint. The way you treat your family, the way you speak to the barista in the coffee shop, the way you advocate for yourself (or don't)...that's all legacy. You're already creating a legacy, whether you're intentional about it or not. So why not get intentional? Think about someone you deeply admire. Not just someone successful, but someone who left a lasting impact on you. Was it what they built? Or was it who they were?

Yes, we remember people for their accomplishments. But more than that, we remember their energy, their courage, and the way they made us feel. This is living a legacy. The impact you create now in your daily actions, your choices, and your presence is what makes the lasting difference. And here's the truth: If you don't design your legacy, you live it by default. So what are you choosing?

The Ripple Effect of Reinvention: What Happens When Women Say Yes to Themselves

Most women underestimate their impact. They ask, "Who am I to change the world?" But the truth is, your energy already is. When you heal, rise, and lead with purpose...you create a ripple that touches generations. That's the work I do. I'm not just a coach. I'm a Legacy Doula, and these women are living proof:

Catherine Curry-Williams

When we met, Catherine Curry Williams was already an accomplished changemaker who turned her pain into purpose. She founded Shane's Inspiration in honor of her late son, Shane, and more recently, the She Angels Foundation, which funds women's charities. Despite her success, Catherine had reached a midlife crossroads where she felt uninspired and unsure of her next move. But after some deep work together, Catherine discovered her legacy and realized that she could make an even greater impact by stepping out of the shadows of midlife and taking the stage.

After taking some of my classes and being a part of the Wise Women Collective Mastermind, Catherine became a powerhouse for change, launching bigger philanthropic initiatives, writing a number-one-best-selling book, and delivering a TEDx talk on transforming pain into purpose.

She's not just healing, she's changing lives. **Her legacy has been activated.**

Kasi Beaney

Kasi, a top level sales executive, had a life that on the surface seemed perfect, but when we first spoke she admitted she was drowning. Kasi was overwhelmed by long, unfulfilling work days, challenging friendship dynamics, parenting teenagers, and sustaining a long-term marriage. She decided to enroll in my six-month program, Limitless. On day one she started making shifts, realizing what needed to change, and now had a community of women to support her. Now as a member of the Wise Women Collective Mastermind, she's launching her own business, a podcast, and is redefining her relationships and feeling more free.

She felt the call to serve on a soul level, launching a coaching business that helps teens and young adults find clarity, confidence, and career direction. Her podcast, *Your Soulful Career Calling*, debuted in 2025, amplifying a message the next generation *desperately needs*. **Her legacy has been put in motion.**

Mindie Antebi

Mindie came to me unsure of exactly what she needed. She was burnt out from a long career in nursing. She was living with a man she loved, but was unsure about the future, and she was struggling with parenting her neurodivergent daughter and dealing with tough family dynamics of blending families and cultures. Through our deep work together in my Limitless program, and as a member of the Wise Women Collective Mastermind, she was able to heal deep trauma from her childhood, and in the process, help her daughter heal. Mindie redefined her relationship with her partner and built a deep connection, one that led to getting married. Learning to love herself fully and stepping into the truth of her wholeness helped her step fully into the spotlight. Mindie reclaimed her voice, transformed her relationships, and found the courage to launch her podcast *Call the Nurse*, creating space for healing, storytelling, and advocacy through media. She's no longer unsure, she has direction. She's leading. **Her legacy has been claimed.**

What do these women have in common? They didn't wait to be perfect. They didn't wait to feel "ready." They chose to lead from their truth, and trusted me to guide them there. This is the ripple effect of deep reinvention. When one woman heals, the world shifts. And this? This is just the beginning.

Your Life's Work: Passion, Purpose, and Impact

If you could be remembered for one thing, what would it be? Not just what you did; but how you made people feel? Your life's work doesn't have to be a single career, a singular achievement, or a perfect plan. It's an intersection:

- Passion – What lights you up, what energizes you, what you care about.
- Purpose – The unique way you serve others and contribute to the world.
- Impact – The ripple effect of your choices, your energy, and how you show up.

Your legacy is built one decision at a time. So, what's your next one?

Guided Reflection: Write Your Living Legacy Statement

Take five minutes and write your Living Legacy statement.

- If you could be remembered for ONE thing, what would it be?
- How do you want people to describe the energy you brought into the world?
- What's one small, intentional action you can take today to live in alignment with that legacy?

Write it. Read it. And then, most importantly-live it. Your legacy starts today. *Are you ready?*

=

At the end of your life, what do you want to look back on and feel? Regret? Or deep, soul-level fulfillment? Because here's the truth: You are building your legacy every single day with the way you live, the choices you make, and the energy you bring into the world. The question is- are you being intentional about it? Because the truth is, your legacy starts now. Not later. Not someday. Now. And if you're ready to step into the fullest, boldest, most limitless version of yourself...it's time to become her. Ready to get started? Find out more at www.lizsvatek.com/limitless

Chapter 10

Becoming HER – Limitless and Unstoppable: Your Next Era

"If you're ready to change your life, stop dragging the past into your present. Start living like HER, the bold, unstoppable woman you're becoming. She's not waiting for permission. She is the permission. Show up as her now... and watch the ripple effect."

It was a difficult beginning. There was pressure to figure it out, force things, and act like everything was "fine". These words- figuring it out, forcing, and fine- are my three least favorite "F words." I was searching for harmony. That feeling when your life is moving with you not against you. When things feel aligned and exciting. But I was treading lightly, because my past showed me that it wasn't safe to have a harmonious life. All I knew was chaos, and so I created more and more of it. Not to punish myself, though it felt that way, but to heal myself. I kept searching for community and sisterhood, but knew I needed something else. Meeting Brett was a mutual attraction. Not just of two people who wanted to create something new, but two people wanting to heal.

Through Brett I learned I was the problem and the solution. He stood up for me until I learned to stand up for myself. I can remember when we almost didn't make it. We wanted to blame the other person for our unhappiness. We wanted it all to be someone else's fault. We felt like life was one continual breech birth. Infertility, family dynamics, Landon's birth, financial stress. It would have been so much easier to just give up, blame each other, and blame circumstances, rather than doing the deep work of facing ourselves and seeing what we didn't want to see.

We tried to make each other the reason we weren't following our dreams, and the reason we were not exploring our legacy. Instead we stood in the deep river of ourselves. This meant addressing the past, our deepest fears, and opening our hearts. Radical personal responsibility shows us that we are responsible for it all, and that's a powerful place to create from. From there, anything is possible. We started following our intuition, our dreams, and our highest expression of ourselves. And great abundance began to show up, and it showed up everywhere. It was there all along. We just couldn't see it.

Just like I realized at forty-nine, there's a version of you out there, who stopped waiting, stopped doubting, and stopped playing small. She owns her power. She walks with confidence. She creates the life she wants without apology. *She is you.* The only difference between her and where you are now? **She decided.** There was no grand moment where the skies opened up and the universe handed her a permission slip. No secret formula, no magical timing, no waiting until she "felt ready." She didn't wake up one morning suddenly more capable, more confident, and more worthy. She just chose.

The biggest lie we've been sold is that confidence comes before action, and that we need to feel sure, feel ready, and feel fearless before we can take the next step. But that's backwards. Confidence isn't a prerequisite for action, it's a byproduct of it. You don't become powerful by waiting to feel powerful. You become her by *acting* as her. You become her by making the choice, over and over again, to move as the woman you want to be, even before she fully arrives. This is the secret of every wildly successful, deeply fulfilled, and truly unstoppable woman. She didn't wait for the feeling. She didn't wait for the certainty. She just decided. And the decision changed everything.

When I was an actress, living in New York in my twenties, I was fascinated with how performers could embody a character. I would watch the great actors and actresses in action and study them, people like Meryl Streep, for example. Meryl Streep is the queen of embodiment. Whether in *Sophie's Choice*, *Silkwood*, *Bridges of Madison County*, or even *The Devil Wears Prada*, we don't see Meryl, we see the character she assumes. She thinks of the way that character talks, walks, thinks, breathes, and lives, and she becomes that. She assumes the character's identity. We forget about Meryl and we believe she is the character she is playing.

In acting classes, I remember loving the process of embodying whatever character I was playing. I thought about her walk, her accent, and what she did when no one was watching. I use those same skills now. I embody what my future self is doing, feeling, and thinking. When I am scared to expand my business or myself, I have to rely on this future me to make the decisions.

What would SHE do?

If you want to change your life, you have to change how you see yourself. Because your identity, who you believe you are, shapes every action you take.

Think about it:

- A woman who sees herself as powerful makes powerful decisions.
- A woman who believes she is worthy doesn't settle.
- A woman who knows she is limitless doesn't hold herself back.

=

It's not about "faking it until you make it." It's about choosing, right now, to operate from your future self's energy.

Ask yourself:

- What would she do today?
- How would she move through her life?
- What boundaries would she enforce?
- What risks would she take?
- What would she stop tolerating?

Go do that!

The Identity Shift Formula

Every single transformation follows the same formula:

- Thoughts → How you think about yourself shapes what you believe is possible.
- Feelings → Your thoughts create your emotions, dictating how you show up.
- Actions → Your emotions influence your behavior and choices.
- Reality → Your actions determine the life you create.

When you shift your thoughts and beliefs about yourself, you shift everything. This is how you become limitless. Not by waiting. Not by hoping. Not by wishing. By choosing, believing, and moving.

Daily Rituals for a Limitless Life

There is no world where you heal a part of you and you're done. You need daily rituals and practices to keep you aligned and moving forward in your life with clarity. Daily rituals aren't just routines, they're anchors. In a world that constantly pulls us out of ourselves, rituals are how we come home. They create a rhythm of safety in the body, a sense of trust in the mind, and a reconnection to the soul. Whether it's five minutes of breathwork, tapping, journaling, or simply placing your hand on your heart and checking in with your body, these practices remind you that you're safe now, and that you're not in survival anymore. And when the nervous system feels safe, that's when true freedom becomes possible. That's when you stop reacting and start creating. That's when you stop performing and start being. Rituals are the way we gently rewire our lives, one sacred moment at a time.

Becoming HER isn't about a one-time breakthrough. It's about consistent, intentional choices. Small, daily rituals that rewire your brain and realign your energy. Here are some of the habits I swear by:

- Morning Power Hour: Start your day with intention- meditation, journaling, movement.
- Embodiment Practices: Walk, talk, and show up as your future self NOW.
- Radical Self-Trust: Make decisions fast. Don't overthink. Your intuition knows.
- Release What No Longer Fits: If it drains you, dims you, or keeps you small-it's done.
- Daily Expansion: Read. Learn. Surround yourself with women who are playing bigger.

When you commit to showing up as *her* every day, the shift happens. And suddenly, you are her. I never set out to be a healer, a leader, or a woman who helps other women rise. I just kept following the next right steps. At every crossroads, I had a choice: Go back to my old patterns, my old stories, and my old limits, or take the leap, trust myself, and keep going. And every time I chose to expand, my life expanded with me. This is how you become the woman who changes everything- by refusing to stay the same.

=

If you want to make your present better, you have to make your future bigger. You have to hold a vision that stretches beyond your current circumstances, beyond the limitations of your past, and beyond what anyone around you has ever done. Because there is often no evidence in your current reality of what's truly possible for you. Vision isn't about proof, it's about permission. It's choosing to believe in something you can't see yet, and showing up for it anyway. When you create from vision, not circumstance, you begin to shift the energy of your life. You make decisions from expansion, not fear. And little by little, your present begins to rise to meet the future you've already claimed.

Visioning Exercise

Write a vision for how you want your life to look. How do you want to feel everyday? What is the legacy you want to live now? What does a day in your new life look like? Who is the future version of you? How does she walk, speak, make decisions, and take up space?

Key Takeaways

- You Already Are Her- The version of you you're chasing isn't out there, she's inside you. Lean in!
- Decisions Create Identity- Every time you act and make decisions from your future self, you become her.
- Confidence Comes from Action, Not Waiting- Clarity and certainty come after you start. Take action!
- Your Life is Yours to Design- No more waiting. No more excuses. No more permission-seeking. You are your own validation and permission.
- The Clock is Ticking- Go all In! If not now, when?

You Are HER. Now Act Like It!

She was never out of reach. She was always inside you. The only thing standing between you and her is a choice. This is your book. This is your legacy. This is your revolution.

And today, you decide.

Journaling Exercise:

As your roles shift and space opens, you are being invited, not just to let go, but to come home to yourself. Take a moment, light a candle, place a hand on your heart, and ask: What am I reclaiming now that I'm no longer needed in the same way? Let whatever comes rise gently.

It might be your voice, your creativity, your sexuality, your ambition, or your joy. Or maybe it's all of it! No answer is too big or too small. This is the beginning of your next legacy.

Chapter 11
Through the Fire

Through the fire, to the limit, to the wall, for a chance to be
with you. I'd gladly risk it all. Through the fire, through
whatever, come what may, for a chance at loving you. I'd take
it all the way, right down to the wire, even through the fire.

- CHAKA KHAN

When Landon was fourteen-months old, I decided to start a mom blog, *One Fabulous Mom*. I was longing for community, a space to lead from the bench, and a way to heal people like me. I wanted them to know that no matter what they were dealing with, they could feel fabulous. I wanted to know that, too. Here's my first post.

I am One Fabulous Mom or at least I try! It's hard to hold it all together and manage to have a little style and class! Being a mom, we all strive to do the best for our kids, but I think there's a way to do it without going crazy. Yes, there are times when it is sheer insanity, but I think if you can get creative, you can really make this mom thing fun for you and your baby! Being a new mother is the most challenging thing I've ever dealt with. Now that Landon is fourteen-months, I am hitting my stride and I'm eager to share all my secrets with you. I will be doing posts on ways to keep your social life going, baby clothes I love, products I can't live without, and everything else! Of course I would love to know your favorites and secrets as well. If you are a fabulous mom or striving to be, you are a hero and you are doing the hard work! Let me be the first to say: You are one fabulous mom!

Slowly I started telling the real story. I would title these truthful posts, "Not So Fabulous." I was sharing the hard journey of parenting a child with a physical difference. That turned into a platform I called: The Warrior Moms. I was creating content, throwing events, and starting to host intimate gatherings. I knew I wanted something bigger, more impactful, and more meaningful. I wanted sisterhood and community.

Then I realized it was not making any money, and I wanted independence and financial freedom. I started a social media agency, took on clients and partners, and built a business I was proud of, but exhausted by. I let that company go and began consulting and running celebrity social media accounts until I landed in luxury marketing. I was searching for meaning in my work, but I kept hitting a wall. That wall was where the money felt great, but the work felt draining.

Like so many people around the world, when 2020 hit I felt like I was splitting apart. I could no longer hold all the pieces of me together. Suddenly I was swept off the social calendar and did something I'd never done before. I committed to exploring what made me truly feel alive, and healing what was holding me back. The truth of how I was living began to leak out. I couldn't fake it anymore. On the surface no one would have known, but things were not as they seemed. I began to care less about how things looked, and more about how I felt inside.

Looking back at the mosaic of my life, these seemingly random fragments made a gorgeous picture of life. I realize now it all makes sense. I can connect the dots when I look backwards, and see the path illuminated before me. I can see the path of legacy. At forty-nine I stopped working and started the *Conversations with Warrior Women Podcast* just as the pandemic hit. The first episode was released on my fiftieth birthday as a gift to myself.

During the pandemic I discovered my life's work. I found out how much I loved the work of transforming myself and other people. When I decided to certify as a coach I was excited, but I had a deep-seated belief that I couldn't make money doing it. I owned the beliefs I adopted when I saw my father's financial failure, and my mother not living her dream. I found the tools to change my beliefs, my thoughts, and actions. I took the leap into entrepreneurship, something I had loved since I was five-years old. I started with mastermind groups, then classes, then retreats. I let myself feel through my business; I had to learn what felt energizing and exciting to offer. There was no "figuring it out," I was *feeling* it out. I learned from everyone I could, and instead of reinventing the wheel, I stole hubcaps. I took pieces of what I saw working for other people and made them my own. In that first year, I had a six-figure business.

I had no clue how I was doing what I was doing. I didn't plan or anticipate having that level of success, but I kept going. I felt the fear, and I used it as fuel. I kept trusting my intuition. That belief that I couldn't make money faded away and I remembered the little girl who started a clowning and magic business in the fifth grade. The one that had a babysitting business in sixth grade. The one that always loved the sound of a cash register since she was a toddler. I remembered the girl with the Donny and Marie Osmond microphone, who would not just sing, but perform. I was a showman, a host, and a speaker. I loved the microphone and speaking passionately. I remembered the girl who loved her pink Barbie dreamhouse, complete with an elevator, and how expansive and limitless that three story dream house was. Barbie could afford anything she wanted and was unapologetic about her pink palace.

I have been passionate about how human beings transform themselves, and my own growth and evolution since I can remember. In writing this book I found journals full of Tony Robbins notes alongside passionate declarations of wanting to trust myself, have a bigger impact,

=

and create a life I loved. I come from a long line of Warrior Women who have sustained themselves, and lived joyfully and with purpose, despite incredible odds.

Like many great women, the stories of their triumphs are not written down anywhere, but told and shared woman-to-woman. I could tell you about my paternal grandmother who was Born in Cardiff, Wales on February 10, 1919. She served in the Cardiff Fire Department during the bombing of the Cardiff dock yards in World War II. She married a Captain in the United States Army and arrived in the United States on the Queen Mary as a war bride. I could also tell you she spent her wedding night alone because her groom was drunk, and that she barely survived the trip over on the Queen Mary. I could tell you when she arrived in the United States, with a trunk of broken china, the only possessions she had, her groom laughed about it.

I could tell you that my maternal grandmother, "Grandmommmie," was devastated from the loss of her husband at just sixty-two-years old, but spoke about him every day after he was gone like he was still alive. She was a well known artist in her community, and also one of the few women that went to college in the 1940s. She continued her education after my grandfather's death, officially graduating from college in her sixties.

History is important, but the backstory is even more important. My parting words every week on my podcast for a long time were, "Every woman has a story, you just need to ask her." And that is still true. But the stories we tell ourselves can make us, or break us. They can catapult us forward or keep us stuck in the past. I started a podcast at the age of fifty and I had no clue what I was doing. I just followed the feeling in my gut, trusting that it would guide me out of the unhappiness and unfulfillment that was overwhelming me.

At forty-nine life was starting to shift, but something inside me was *still* breaking down, crying out, wanting depth and purpose. I had been living my life letting outside circumstances determine my choices. I made choices based on what other people told me, or how they saw me, or how I wanted to be seen. I could no longer find my own internal compass because I had thrown it away time and time again. I was physically exhausted. But mostly, I was tired of myself and the choices I was making. I was tired of the way I was living.

I watched women coming into their fifties feeling sad and uninspired. It alarmed me. It was like turning fifty was a kind of reckoning where everything you ever accomplished was added up, and everyone felt like they were falling short. So, with my husband's support, I took a pause. I stopped everything; work, socializing, the busyness and spinning, so I could actually feel something. And boy, did I start to feel something. I knew I had been betraying myself in so many ways, not taking care of myself and allowing unhealthy dynamics in friendships and family to continue to wear me down. I started to put up boundaries, and when I did, it was like a planned explosion.

I watched these massive buildings that had stood for years, that I thought were permanent, come down. I didn't know things could be different. I thought I had to endure, that these were my rocks to carry. I didn't know that I could choose. That I could be different. Soon the air was clear. The sky was blue. Suddenly I could hear my intuition again. I could hear my voice, and I felt lighter.

I know now that when I started creating the podcast, I was finally present. I was in the moment, challenged, and taking a risk. I felt...*alive*. And it wasn't until I was feeling alive that I knew that for years I had been dead. Numb. Just going through the motions of life. Riding the rollercoaster of motherhood, marriage, work, and friends. I was on a hamster wheel going nowhere. When I had taken that pause and started the podcast, the hamster wheel stopped and I took a look around and realized where I was.

=

The podcast became a way for me to express myself, to learn about myself, and to expand myself. I thought of naming the podcast, *Drinking in the Driveway*. I was thinking about that moment when women pull in the driveway and sometimes, pause. They pause before going inside because they know once they walk in the door it's back to the routine. Back to reality. At that time, my kids were eleven and thirteen. Motherhood was feeling less about survival mode but even so, most of the moms I knew, including myself, were just looking to get to the wine at the end of the night. So *Drinking in the Driveway* seemed like a good idea for a title, and it was something I used to joke about with my busy, tired, working mom friends.

But as I started to record the first few episodes, I realized it was way more than that. Women were sharing deeply painful stories and how they managed to stay afloat. They were telling stories of tragedy to triumph, pain to purpose, and so *Conversations with Warrior Women* became the title. These women were sharing their stories because they knew it would pull another woman out of whatever she was going through, and it was so powerful.

Despite the devastation of the world mentally and physically throughout the pandemic, I found myself thriving because I finally had the stillness I craved. My friends helped me celebrate my fiftieth birthday with a magnificent parade. I cried my eyes out as friends and family drove by dancing, honking, singing with signs and streamers, and blasting my favorite songs on their radios. They blew kisses and brought gifts. It was such a blessing.

The first episode of *Conversations with Warrior Women* aired the next day, April 15th, 2020. My first guest was my dear friend JoAnne Lord who talked candidly about her breast cancer battle. As the first episodes started to air, and the pandemic wore on, I found myself in sheer bliss. I was off the social calendar and totally immersed in finding compelling guests, having deep connective conversations, and planning episodes. I was learning so much from these women. The friends I interviewed were vulnerable and it brought us closer. My husband was listening in from the other room, amazed at what I was doing. My kids were excited for me, and I was starting to build a listenership.

I became more confident in my voice, more adept at interviewing, and started to reach out for bigger guests. I reached out to my friend Hillary Gadsby of Boss Talks Networks and asked to interview her. She was kind enough to reach into her contacts and connect me to incredible women. One of the women she suggested was Tracy Litt and on March 10th, 2021 I was changed forever. After hearing Tracy explain that thoughts were "just options," and how you aren't able to make decisions when you're too much in your "humanness," I was stunned speechless. Then she said, "You can't desire something if it's not already yours, the wanting of it tells you that it's already available to you. You just need to get into alignment, so that it can show up and you can produce it." *Boom.*

Something hit there. She was offering me thoughts and ways of explaining things I had never considered. I was intrigued, but I went back to business as usual. I was feeling pretty good about the podcast and my new boundaries, but when my good friend from college, Pam Rogers, told me she loved my episode with Tracy and she was going to go to her retreat in Palm Beach, I wanted to know more. Pam had done an even deeper dive on Tracy and wanted to see her live. I decided to join her. That one decision changed everything. We were still in the mess of the pandemic which made me nervous, but I decided to go anyway and brought my new friend Amy Young along with me. She and I were reinventing together. We still are.

At that retreat I had several spiritual awakenings with Tracy. Later that weekend I met Vaughn Pierro. Through her "Holy Breath Method", I was able to see that I really was a Warrior Woman. I saw I was supposed to be leading women, coaching women, and healing women. The podcast was only the beginning. I signed up with Tracy to certify as a coach and spent the next year learning from her and the amazing women in my cohort. Tracy taught mindset and transformation using examples from her life, she let us see behind the curtain, and it let us all know we could do it too. My confidence was rising, and so I boldly started mastermind groups for women, before I was ready. Beginning before I was "ready" has been one of the secrets of my success.

The chemistry in these groups was electric. I led them through experiences and coached them from what I intuitively knew they needed. I had learned such wisdom from the podcast, and all the personal growth work I had done over the years, and once I was certified as a coach, it felt even more aligned.

Finally all the things in my life started to make sense. All the things I had done over the years from acting, and writing, and stand up comedy, to social media and marketing and brand building. I was using everything I ever learned. Even my experience as a mom and a wife....as a Warrior Woman...all of it had relevance. All of those experiences held wisdom and needed to be shared. The women in the mastermind started to trust their intuition and wisdom, too. I was going through a powerful evolution where I was stepping into my legacy and was leading women to do the same.

The personal development I was doing was unlike anything I'd done before. It seemed like every week I was upleveling, letting go, shedding the skin of my old self, and becoming new. After I launched the mastermind groups I developed my signature program called Limitless. I loved teaching the work that had changed my life so drastically. I watched as women embraced the tools, as well as my brand of humor and healing.

The more I saw women transform, the more curious I became about the path of healing and transformation. I wanted to know why some women choose it and others don't. Why were some women embracing life after forty while others were sadder than ever? I wanted to understand how some women could not heal past deep traumas that they spent their whole lives trying to manage. I was reading, researching, learning different modalities, when I discovered Marissa Peer and Rapid Transformational Therapy. When I saw the results that were possible I knew immediately I wanted to become certified to use this tool in my own coaching. The sessions I had were life changing and results were immediate. I knew every woman needed this. I spent another year getting that certification. And when I discovered Human Design, I realized I'd finally found the recipe for Legacy.

When I started *Conversations with Warrior Women* I didn't know what I was truly capable of. I didn't know what my legacy was. I didn't believe I could launch a business and make more money than I ever had before as a coach. I didn't even think anyone would listen to the podcast at all. But now I'm not just a Rapid Transformational Therapist, I'm a healer who's helped hundreds of women using my Warrior Soul Healing Method.

You can check it out here: www.lizsvatek.com/rtt

I'm a Human Design expert who shows women the path to their purpose. And now, my award-winning podcast is listened to in fifty-seven countries and has been downloaded 157,385 times. Yes, I made six-figures my first year in business but I have doubled and tripled that year over year. As I am writing this book in 2025, my business has increased by 147 percent.

I've been called the Taylor Swift of midlife by some clients, and the Mel Robbins for women over forty by others. All I know is that I am the woman who can see the legacy in every woman I work with. I take women from mindfuckery to magic through Warrior Soul Healing, little girl work, tangible tools and practices and a huge dose of humor. I build collectives of women from across the country who know the power of

=

listening to their sisters and holding space for their emotions without judgement. I teach them how to extract the diamonds of wisdom from even the darkest times in their lives. I lift the weight of trauma off of women so they can soar, and through this work I continue, every single day, to heal from my own trauma and subconscious blocks.

I help women create their own unique impact and legacy as I create my own. I have a clear mission now; to heal one million women. I have a vision where I travel across the country filling stadiums where women bring their friends, daughters, and mothers, and we laugh, heal, and transform. It's the women's empowerment superbowl, where we create an army of women who are living their legacy in this world and pulling other women forward. I am encouraging the women I coach to play bigger. These women are already incredibly accomplished and successful, and yet I know there's more for them. If I'm going to ask the women I'm working with to trust more and leap, I have to take leaps and play bigger in my life, too. That means the launch of *The Liz Svatek Show* on YouTube. And a Ted Talk. And this book.

It's not just fitting that I step into the spotlight now, at this age - **it's destined.** This season of my life is the one I've been waiting for and dreaming of. I've earned this voice- through fire, through grace, and through every scar I once tried to hide. I've gathered the wisdom. I've claimed the strength. And now, I'm standing in the full force of my intuitive power.

Let me be clear: I know exactly what I'm here to do. I'm not just building a legacy. I'm igniting a movement. And, dear Warrior Woman, I'm not going alone. I'm inviting you. No, I'm calling you into this next level and new era with me.

Because this isn't just my ascension. It's *ours.*

And so the end of this book is a new beginning. Because we always have the chance to begin again. We always have a chance to be brand new, and to meet each other from a different place...a higher perspective. We all have the power to get up on the roof of our lives and look around. And from the roof you'll soon see that nothing is happening to you. It's all happening for you...and if you climb a little higher, you'll see it's happening through you. Because when you lean into wisdom, when you start to believe in the magic of you....you become it. I've seen it happen over and over again. That magic is real, and it's all within you. I want you to imagine that right now there are hundreds and thousands of women reading this book, feeling the way you feel. They are ready to cheer you on and watch you live your legacy. Now you have a whole community of Warrior Women to support you.

I was parentified at a young age- made to carry the emotional weight that my parents couldn't hold themselves. I became the fixer, the comedian, and the one who made everything okay. Somewhere along the way, I internalized the belief that my worth was tied to how well I could solve other people's problems. I believed that if I could just keep everyone else afloat, maybe I'd finally feel safe, seen, or loved. But no matter how hard I tried, I couldn't fix them. I believed that if I could just make everything okay for everyone else, I would finally be safe. Seen. Chosen. So I made myself indispensable, intuitive, and endlessly capable. I learned to anticipate needs before they were spoken. I learned that my worth was measured in how well I could hold everyone else together.

But here's the heartache of it: I couldn't fix them. Not my parents. Not the chaos. Not the unspoken pain that hovered like smoke in our home. And for a long time, that made me feel like I had failed. Like I was the problem. It wasn't until I began to heal, the real kind of healing, the kind that rewires your cells and reclaims your voice, that I realized something powerful:

=

I was never meant to fix them. I was meant to free myself. And every woman reading this book. And in that freedom, I discovered something else: **My legacy was waiting on the other side of my healing.** The work I was born to do didn't come from ease- it was carved from pain, conviction, and the fires I walked through and refused to let define me.

My Human Design confirmed what I always knew in my bones: I'm here to see deeply into people, to guide them to embrace a new identity, and reclaim their joy. Not because I read it in a book, but because I *lived* it. That is the most sacred kind of purpose; one forged in personal truth. Legacy isn't something you leave behind. It's something you build while you're still here. It's birthed through the wounds you refuse to ignore, the patterns you choose to break, and the gifts you finally claim as your own. And that's what I've done. I've turned my pain into power, my healing into a roadmap, and my story into service. This is my legacy, and if you're reading this, you're holding the invitation to discover yours, too.

When I began writing this book I went on a retreat to Florida. It was going to be the jumping off point. On the flight over I must have written fifty pages. I was so excited about delving in. I had carved out this time. Landon had just gone through another surgery on his arm and it was incredibly successful on so many levels. First because he chose to do it after a surgery that had gone wrong years ago. He had let go of the pain and arrived at the hospital as an eighteen-year-old man. He walked in alone, made the nurses laugh, and asked them to play Playboi Carti during surgery. All this from a kid who used to have so much anxiety before all his surgeries he would throw up. The surgery was incredibly successful with Dr. Kulber (our hero) being able to get more mobility in his arm than ever before. The second part of the surgery would happen six weeks later, and Landon chose to schedule it during my retreat. "I've got this Mom, you go write your book."

I arrived in Florida ready to write. Landon had his second surgery and it was successful. After twenty-four hours in Florida, I got word about fires in Los Angeles. At first this seemed to be nowhere near our home, and something they could contain. But the fire spread quickly and became a monster unlike anything we had ever seen. Brett decided to bring the kids and dogs to my sister-in-law Rachel's house, mainly because Landon was healing from his skin grafting. I felt the pull to go home and be with them, but my husband assured me he had it covered. I stayed and wrote and tried to not watch the news twenty-four hours a day. The fire got bigger and bigger, but I watched as my family pulled together, encouraging me to stay where I was. I leaned into trust, that I was where I was supposed to be. The next morning Landon texted me he was in extreme pain, something was wrong with his arm. I booked my ticket and flew home. The fires seemed to be away from our home when I landed, but once I got to my sister-in-law's house the winds had changed.

Brett and I nervously drove to our house to grab baby books, photo albums, art by my grandmother and mother, and anything else we could think of. We watched the giant, ominous plume of smoke from the highway, and when we got to our neighborhood it was silent. Everyone was gone. We walked in the house, a plume of smoke rising in the distance in the backyard, helicopters circling, and my body went numb. I was frozen in fear and almost unable to move. It was the same way I felt when I was little and I was afraid of my father. I breathed deeply, got back in my body, and forced myself to move and quickly grab what we needed. We drove back to my sister-in-law's in shock. Days went by where we were under constant threat of losing our home. It was hard to think of anything, let alone writing this book. With other natural disasters there is an end. This seemed to be endless. The fire had grown to record-breaking levels, and soon the Pacific Palisades was gone. The restaurants and parks and shops in Malibu where we had spent so much time together as a

=

family...everything was ash. After the fires we went home, but we weren't the same. So many people lost everything. The landscape of our lives was totally different. I found myself even more convicted about what I am here to do.

Living in Los Angeles is not for the faint of heart. Every year, the hills blaze. Smoke rises. Ash falls like snow. And yet...the most extraordinary thing happens after the fire. **Life returns.** The earth, scorched and blackened, quietly begins to bloom again. Seeds that only open in heat awaken. Green pushes through the ash. Beauty returns- not in spite of the fire, but because of it. And I can't help but think: **We are the same.**

We are the phoenix. Burned. Broken open. Brought to our knees, but never destroyed. We rise. Again, and again, and again. And each time, we have a choice: To stay buried in the ashes of what was...Or to rise into who we're here to become. This book wasn't written for the woman who wants to stay the same. It was written for the woman who knows she is made for *more.*

It was written for the woman who feels the fire within her, and who is ready to build something that lasts, not just for her, but for every woman who comes after.

This is your invitation to legacy. Not the kind measured in money or monuments, but in healing, truth, joy, and generational transformation. You are not behind. You are not too late. You are right on time. And this season? This season is your season. This isn't your ending.

This is your rising. And it starts right now.

As a thank you for making it to the end of this book, I want to offer you a 20-minute discovery call to see if coaching with me is the right fit for you.

You can book your call using this link:

calendly.com/lizsvatek/midlifeaudit

Book Credits:

Edited by Laura Lindsey
Hair Styling and Makeup by Liz Conde
Photography: Kathy Schuh

Made in United States
Orlando, FL
30 May 2025

61709864R00106